ABRAHAM LINCOLN AND THE UNION:

A CHRONICLE OF

THE EMBATTLED NORTH

ABRAHAM LINCOLN AND THE UNION:

A CHRONICLE OF

THE EMBATTLED NORTH

NATHANIEL W. STEPHENSON

Borgo Military Reference • MMIII

ABRAHAM LINCOLN AND THE UNION:
A CHRONICLE OF THE EMBATTLED NORTH

New elements copyright © 2003 by **Wildside Press.** All rights reserved.
Cover design copyright © 2003 by **JT Lindroos**
Series Editor: Sean Wallace

Wildside Press, LLC
PO Box 301, Holicong, PA 18928-0301
www.wildsidepress.com

ISBN : 0-8095-4452-0 (casebound)
ISBN: 0-8095-4453-9 (paperback)

INDEX

PREFACE		7
I.	THE TWO NATIONS OF THE REPUBLIC	9
II.	THE PARTY OF POLITICAL EVASION	18
III.	THE POLITICIANS AND THE NEW DAY	28
IV.	THE CRISIS	37
V.	SECESSION	48
VI.	WAR	58
VII.	LINCOLN	70
VIII.	THE RULE OF LINCOLN	78
IX.	THE CRUCIAL MATTER	91
X.	THE SECRETARY OF THE TREASURY	103
XI.	NORTHERN LIFE DURING THE WAR	109
XII.	THE MEXICAN EPISODE	119
XIII.	THE PLEBISCITE OF 1864	124
XIV.	LINCOLN'S FINAL INTENTIONS	133
BIBLIOGRAPHICAL NOTE		138

PREFACE

In spite of a lapse of sixty years, the historian who attempts to portray the era of Lincoln is still faced with almost impossible demands and still confronted with arbitrary points of view. It is out of the question, in a book so brief as this must necessarily be, to meet all these demands or to alter these points of view. Interests that are purely local, events that did not with certainty contribute to the final outcome, gossip, as well as the mere caprice of the scholar—these must obviously be set aside.

The task imposed upon the volume resolves itself, at bottom, into just two questions: Why was there a war? Why was the Lincoln Government successful? With these two questions always in mind I have endeavored, on the one hand, to select and consolidate the pertinent facts; on the other, to make clear, even at the cost of explanatory comment, their relations in the historical sequence of cause and effect. This purpose has particularly governed the use of biographical matter, in which the main illustration, of course, is the career of Lincoln. Prominent as it is here made, the Lincoln matter all bears in the last analysis on one point—his control of his support. On that the history of the North hinges. The personal and private Lincoln it is impossible to present within these pages. The public Lincoln, including the character of his mind, is here the essential matter.

The bibliography at the close of the volume indicates the more important books which are at the reader's disposal and which it is unfortunate not to know.

NATHANIEL W. STEPHENSON. Charleston, S. C., March, 1918.

CHAPTER I
THE TWO NATIONS OF THE REPUBLIC

"There is really no Union now between the North and the South... No two nations upon earth entertain feelings of more bitter rancor toward each other than these two nations of the Republic."

This remark, which is attributed to Senator Benjamin Wade of Ohio, provides the key to American politics in the decade following the Compromise of 1850. To trace this division of the people to its ultimate source, one would have to go far back into colonial times. There was a process of natural selection at work, in the intellectual and economic conditions of the eighteenth century, which inevitably drew together certain types and generated certain forces. This process manifested itself in one form in His Majesty's plantations of the North, and in another in those of the South. As early as the opening of the nineteenth century, the social tendencies of the two regions were already so far alienated that they involved differences which would scarcely admit of reconciliation. It is a truism to say that these differences gradually were concentrated around fundamentally different conceptions of labor—of slave labor in the South, of free labor in the North.

Nothing, however, could be more fallacious than the notion that this growing antagonism was controlled by any deliberate purpose in either part of the country. It was apparently necessary that this Republic in its evolution should proceed from confederation to nationality through an intermediate and apparently reactionary period of sectionalism. In this stage of American history, slavery was without doubt one of the prime factors involved, but sectional consciousness, with all its emotional and psychological implications, was the fundamental impulse of the stern events which occurred between 1850 and 1865.

By the middle of the nineteenth century the more influential Southerners had come generally to regard their section of the country as a distinct social unit. The next step was inevitable. The South began to regard itself as a separate political unit. It is the distinction of Calhoun that he showed himself toward the end sufficiently flexible to become the exponent of this new political impulse. With all his earlier fire he encouraged the Southerners to withdraw from the so-called national parties, Whig and Democratic, to establish instead a single Southern party, and to formulate, by means of popular conventions, a single concerted policy for the entire South.

At that time such a policy was still regarded, from the Southern point of view, as a radical idea. In 1851, a battle was fought at the polls between the two Southern ideas—the old one which upheld separate state independence, and the new one which virtually acknowledged Southern nationality. The issue at stake was the acceptance or the rejection of a compromise which could bring no permanent settlement of fundamental differences.

Nowhere was the battle more interesting than in South Carolina, for it brought into clear light that powerful Southern leader who ten years later was to be the masterspirit of secession—Robert Barnwell Rhett. In 1851 he fought hard to revive the older idea of state independence and to carry South Carolina as a separate state out of the Union. Accordingly it is significant of the progress that the consolidation of the South had made at this date that on this issue Rhett encountered general opposition. This difference of opinion as to policy was not inspired, as some historians have too hastily concluded, by national feeling. Scarcely any of the leaders of the opposition considered the Federal Government supreme over the State Government. They opposed Rhett because they felt secession to be at that moment bad policy. They saw that, if South Carolina went out of the Union in 1851, she would go alone and the solidarity of the South would be broken. They were not lacking in sectional patriotism, but their conception of the best solution of the complex problem differed from that advocated by Rhett. Their position was summed up by Langdon Cheves when he said, "To secede now is to secede from the South as well as from the

Union." On the basis of this belief they defeated Rhett and put off secession for ten years.

There is no analogous single event in the history of the North, previous to the war, which reveals with similar clearness a sectional consciousness. On the surface the life of the people seemed, indeed, to belie the existence of any such feeling. The Northern capitalist class aimed steadily at being non-sectional, and it made free use of the word national. We must not forget, however, that all sorts of people talked of national institutions, and that the term, until we look closely into the mind of, the person using it, signifies nothing. Because the Northern capitalist repudiated the idea of sectionalism, it does not follow that he set up any other in its place. Instead of accomplishing anything so positive, he remained for the most part a negative quantity.

Living usually somewhere between Maine and Ohio, he made it his chief purpose to regulate the outflow of manufactures from that industrial region and the inflow of agricultural produce. The movement of the latter eastward and northward, and the former westward and southward, represents roughly but graphically the movement of the business of that time. The Easterner lived in fear of losing the money which was owed him in the South. As the political and economic conditions of the day made unlikely any serious clash of interest between the East and the West, he had little solicitude about his accounts beyond the Alleghanies. But a gradually developing hostility between North and South was accompanied by a parallel anxiety on the part of Northern capital for its Southern investments and debts. When the war eventually became inevitable, $200,000,000 were owed by Southerners to Northerners. For those days this was an indebtedness of no inconsiderable magnitude. The Northern capitalists, preoccupied with their desire to secure this account, were naturally eager to repudiate sectionalism, and talked about national interests with a zeal that has sometimes been misinterpreted. Throughout the entire period from 1850 to 1865, capital in American politics played for the most part a negative role, and not until after the war did it become independent of its Southern interests.

For the real North of that day we must turn to those Northerners who felt sufficient unto themselves and whose political convictions were unbiased by personal interests which were involved in other parts of the country. We must listen to the distinct voices that gave utterance to their views, and we must observe the definite schemes of their political leaders.

Directly we do this, the fact stares us in the face that the North had become a democracy. The rich man no longer played the role of grandee, for by this time there had arisen those two groups which, between them, are the ruin of aristocracy—the class of prosperous laborers and the group of well-to-do intellectuals. Of these, the latter gave utterance, first, to their faith in democracy, and then, with all the intensity of partisan zeal, to their sense of the North as the agent of democracy. The prosperous laborers applauded this expression of an opinion in which they thoroughly believed and at the same time gave their willing support to a land policy that was typically Northern.

American economic history in the middle third of the century is essentially the record of a struggle to gain possession of public land. The opposing forces were the South, which strove to perpetuate by this means a social system that was fundamentally aristocratic, and the North, which sought by the same means to foster its ideal of democracy. Though the South, with the aid of its economic vassal, the Northern capitalist class, was for some time able to check the land-hunger of the Northern democrats, it was never able entirely to secure the control which it desired, but was always faced with the steady and continued opposition of the real North. On one occasion in Congress, the heart of the whole matter was clearly shown, for at the very moment when the Northerners of the democratic class were pressing one of their frequent schemes for free land, Southerners and their sympathetic Northern henchmen were furthering a scheme that aimed at the purchase of Cuba. From the impatient sneer of a Southerner that the Northerners sought to give "land to the landless" and the retort that the Southerners seemed equally anxious to supply "niggers to the niggerless," it can be seen that American history is sometimes better summed up by angry politicians than by historians.

We must be on our guard, however, against ascribing to either side too precise a consciousness of its own motives. The old days when the American Civil War was conceived as a clear-cut issue are as a watch in the night that has passed, and we now realize that historical movements are almost without exception the resultants of many motives. We have come to recognize that men have always misapprehended themselves, contradicted themselves, obeyed primal impulses, and then deluded themselves with sophistications upon the springs of action. In a word, unaware of what they are doing, men allow their aesthetic and dramatic senses to shape their conceptions of their own lives.

That "great impersonal artist," of whom Matthew Arnold has so much to say, is at work in us all, subtly making us into illusions, first to ourselves and later to the historian. It is the business of history, as of analytic fiction, both to feel the power of these illusions and to work through them in imagination to the dim but potent motives on which they rest. We are prone to forget that we act from subconscious quite as often as from conscious influences, from motives that arise out of the dim parts of our being, from the midst of shadows that psychology has only recently begun to lift, where senses subtler than the obvious make use of fear, intuition, prejudice, habit, and illusion, and too often play with us as the wind with blown leaves.

True as this is of man individually, it is even more fundamentally true of man collectively, of parties, of peoples. It is a strikingly accurate description of the relation of the two American nations that now found themselves opposed within the Republic. Neither fully understood the other. Each had a social ideal that was deeper laid than any theory of government or than any commercial or humanitarian interest. Both knew vaguely but with sure instinct that their interests and ideals were irreconcilable. Each felt in its heart the deadly passion of self-preservation. It was because, in both North and South, men were subtly conscious that a whole social system was the issue at stake, and because on each side they believed in their own ideals with their whole souls, that, when the time came for their trial by fire, they went to their deaths singing.

In the South there still obtained the ancient ideal of territorial aristocracy. Those long traditions of the Western European peoples which had made of the great landholder a petty prince lay beneath the plantation life of the Southern States. The feudal spirit, revived in a softer world and under brighter skies, gave to those who participated in it the same graces and somewhat the same capacities which it gave to the knightly class in the days of Roland—courage, frankness, generosity, ability in affairs, a sense of responsibility, the consciousness of caste. The mode of life which the planters enjoyed and which the inferior whites regarded as a social paradise was a life of complete deliverance from toil, of disinterested participation in local government, of absolute personal freedom—a life in which the mechanical action of law was less important than the more human compulsion of social opinion, and in which private differences were settled under the code of honor.

This Southern life was carried on in the most appropriate environment.

On a landed estate, often larger than many of Europe's baronies, stood the great house of the planter, usually a graceful example of colonial architecture, surrounded by stately gardens. This mansion was the center of a boundless hospitality; guests were always coming and going; the hostess and her daughters were the very symbols of kindliness and ease. To think of such houses was to think of innumerable joyous days; of gentlemen galloping across country after the hounds; of coaches lumbering along avenues of noble oaks, bringing handsome women to visit the mansion; of great feastings; of nights of music and dancing; above all, of the great festival of Christmas, celebrated much as had been the custom in "Merrie England" centuries before.

Below the surface of this bright world lay the enslaved black race. In the minds of many Southerners—it was always a secret burden from which they saw no means of freeing themselves. To emancipate the slaves, and thereby to create a population of free blacks, was generally considered, from the white point of view, an impossible solution of the problem. The Southerners usually believed that the African could be tamed only in small groups and when constantly surrounded by white influence, as in the case of house servants. Though a few great capitalists had taken up the idea that the deliberate exploitation of the blacks was the high prerogative of the whites, the general sentiment of the Southern people was more truly expressed by Toombs when he said: "The question is not whether we could be more prosperous and happy with these three and a half million slaves in Africa, and their places filled with an equal number of hardy, intelligent, and enterprising citizens of the superior race; but it is simply whether, while we have them among us, we would be most prosperous with them in freedom or in bondage."

The Southern people, in the majority of instances, had no hatred of the blacks. In the main they led their free, spirited, and gracious life, convinced that the maintenance of slavery was but making the best of circumstances which were beyond their control. It was these Southern people who were to hear from afar the horrible indictment of all their motives by the Abolitionists and who were to react in a growing bitterness and distrust toward everything Northern.

But of these Southern people the average Northerner knew nothing. He knew the South only on its least attractive side of professional politics. For there was a group of powerful magnates, rich planters or "slave barons," who easily made their way into Congress, and who played into the hands of the Northern capitalists, for a purpose similar to theirs. It was these men who forced the issue upon slavery; they warned the common people of the North to mind their own business; and for doing so they were warmly applauded by the Northern capitalist class. It was therefore in opposition to the whole American world of organized capital that the Northern masses demanded the use of "the Northern hammer"—as Sumner put it, in one of his most furious speeches—in their aim to destroy a section where, intuitively, they felt their democratic ideal could not be realized.

And what was that ideal? Merely to answer democracy is to dodge the fundamental question. The North was too complex in its social structure and too multitudinous in its interests to confine itself to one type of life. It included all sorts and conditions of men—from the most gracious of scholars who lived in romantic ease among his German and Spanish books, and whose lovely house in Cambridge is forever associated with the noble presence of Washington, to the hardy frontiersman, breaking the new soil of his Western claim, whose wife at sunset shaded her tired eyes, under a hand rough with labor, as she stood on the threshold of her log cabin, watching for the return of her man across the weedy fields which he had not yet fully subdued. Far apart as were Longfellow and this toiler of the West, they yet felt themselves to be one in purpose.

They were democrats, but not after the simple, elementary manner of the democrats at the opening of the century. In the North, there had come to life a peculiar phase of idealism that had touched democracy with mysticism and had added to it a vague but genuine romance. This new vision of the destiny of the country had the practical effect of making the Northerners identify themselves in their imaginations with all mankind and in creating in them an enthusiastic desire, not only to give to every American a home of his own, but also to throw open the gates of the nation and to share the wealth of America with the poor of all the world. In very truth, it was their dominating passion to give "land to the landless." Here was the clue to much of their attitude toward the South. Most of these Northern dreamers gave little or no thought to slavery itself; but they felt that the section which maintained such a system so committed to aristocracy that any real friendship with it was impossible.

We are thus forced to conceive the American Republic in the years immediately following the Compromise of 1850 as, in effect, a dual nation, without a common loyalty between the two parts. Before long the most significant of the great Northerners of the time was to describe this impossible condition by the appropriate metaphor of a house divided against itself. It was not, however, until eight years after the division of the country had been acknowledged in 1850 that these words were uttered. In those eight years both sections awoke to the seriousness of the differences that they had admitted. Both perceived that, instead of solving their problem in 1850, they had merely drawn sharply the lines of future conflict. In every thoughtful mind there arose the same alternative questions: Is there no solution but fighting it out until one side destroys the other, or we end as two nations confessedly independent? Or is there some conceivable new outlet for this opposition of energy on the part of the sections, some new mode of permanent adjustment?

It was at the moment when thinking men were asking these questions that one of the nimblest of politicians took the center of the stage. Stephen A. Douglas was far-sighted enough to understand the land-hunger of the time. One is tempted to add that his ear was to the ground. The statement will not, however, go unchallenged, for able apologists have their good word to say for Douglas. Though in the main, the traditional view of him as the prince of political jugglers still holds its own, let us admit that his bold, rough spirit, filled as it was with political daring, was not without its strange vein of idealism. And then let us repeat that his ear was to the ground. Much careful research has indeed been expended in seeking to determine who originated the policy which, about 1853, Douglas decided to make his own. There has also been much dispute about his motives. Most of us, however, see in his course of action an instance of playing the game of politics with an audacity that was magnificent.

His conduct may well have been the result of a combination of motives which included a desire to retain the favor of the Northwest, a wish to pave the way to his candidacy for the Presidency, the intention to enlist the aid of the South as well as that of his own locality, and perhaps the hope that he was performing a service of real value to his country. That is, he saw that the favor of his own Northwest would be lavished upon any man who opened up to settlement the rich lands beyond Iowa and Missouri which were still held by the Indians, and for which the Westerners were clamoring. Furthermore, they wanted a railroad that would reach to the Pacific. There were, however, local entanglements and political cross-purposes which involved the interests of the free State of Illinois and those of the slave State of Missouri.

Douglas's great stroke was a programme for harmonizing all these conflicting interests and for drawing together the West and the South. Slaveholders were to be given what at that moment they wanted most—an opportunity to expand into that territory to the north and west of Missouri which had been made free by the Compromise of 1820, while the free Northwest was to have its railroad to the coast and also its chance to expand into the Indian country. Douglas thus became the champion of a bill which would organize two new territories, Kansas and Nebraska, but which would leave the settlers in each to decide whether slavery or free labor should prevail within their boundaries. This territorial scheme was accepted by a Congress in which the Southerners and their Northern allies held control, and what is known as the Kansas-Nebraska Bill was signed by President Pierce on May 30, 1854.[1]

---

[1] The origin of the Kansas-Nebraska Bill has been a much discussed subject among historians in recent years. The older view that Douglas was simply playing into the hands of the "slavepower" by sacrificing Kansas, is no longer tenable. This point has been elaborated by Allen Johnson in his study of Douglas ("Stephen A. Douglas: a Study in American Politics"). In his "Repeal of the Missouri Compromise", P.O. Ray contends that the legislation of 1854 originated in a factional controversy in Missouri, and that Douglas merely served the interests of the proslavery group led by Senator David R. Atchinson of Missouri. Still another point of view is that presented in the "Genesis of the Kansas-Nebraska Act," by F. H. Hodder, who would explain not only the division of the Nebraska Territory into Kansas and Nebraska, but the object of the entire bill by the insistent efforts of promoters of the Pacific railroad scheme to secure a right of way through Nebraska. This project involved the organization of a territorial government and the repeal of the Missouri Compromise. Douglas was deeply interested in the western railroad interests and carried through the necessary legislation.

CHAPTER II.
THE PARTY OF POLITICAL EVASION

In order to understand Douglas one must understand the Democratic party of 1854 in which Douglas was a conspicuous leader. The Democrats boasted that they were the only really national party and contended that their rivals, the Whigs and the Know-Nothings, were merely the representatives of localities or classes. Sectionalism was the favorite charge which the Democrats brought against their enemies; and yet it was upon these very Democrats that the slaveholders had hitherto relied, and it was upon certain members of this party that the label, "Northern men with Southern principles," had been bestowed.

The label was not, however, altogether fair, for the motives of the Democrats were deeply rooted in their own peculiar temperament. In the last analysis, what had held their organization together, and what had enabled them to dominate politics for nearly the span of a generation, was their faith in a principle that then appealed powerfully, and that still appeals, to much in the American character. This was the principle of negative action on the part of the government—the old idea that the government should do as little as possible and should confine itself practically to the duties of the policeman. This principle has seemed always to express to the average mind that traditional individualism which is an inheritance of the Anglo-Saxon race. In America, in the middle of the nineteenth century, it reenforced that tradition of local independence which was strong throughout the West and doubly strong in the South. Then, too, the Democratic party still spoke the language of the theoretical Democracy inherited from Jefferson. And Americans have always been the slaves of phrases!

Furthermore, the close alliance of the Northern party machine with the South made it, generally, an object of care for all those Northern interests that depended on the Southern market. As to the Southerners, their relation with this party has two distinct chapters. The first embraced the twenty years preceding the Compromise of 1850, and may be thought of as merging into the second during three or four years following the great equivocation. In that period, while the antislavery crusade was taking form, the aim of Southern politicians was mainly negative. "Let us alone," was their chief demand. Though aggressive in their policy, they were too far-sighted to demand of the North any positive course in favor of slavery. The rise of a new type of Southern politician, however, created a different situation and began a second chapter in the relation between the South and the Democratic party machine in the North. But of that hereafter.

Until 1854, it was the obvious part of wisdom for Southerners to cooperate as far as possible with that party whose cardinal idea was that the government should come as near as conceivable to a system of non-interference; that it should not interfere with business, and therefore oppose a tariff; that it should not interfere with local government, and therefore applaud states rights; that it should not interfere with slavery, and therefore frown upon militant abolition. Its policy was, to adopt a familiar phrase, one of masterly inactivity. Indeed it may well be called the party of political evasion. It was a huge, loose confederacy of differing political groups, embracing paupers and millionaires, moderate anti-slavery men and slave barons, all of whom were held together by the unreliable bond of an agreement not to tread on each other's toes.

Of this party Douglas was the typical representative, both in strength and weakness. He had all its pliability, its good humor, its broad and easy way with things, its passion for playing politics. Nevertheless, in calling upon the believers in political evasion to consent for this once to reverse their principle and to endorse a positive action, he had taken a great risk. Would their sporting sense of politics as a gigantic game carry him through successfully? He knew that there was a hard fight before him, but with the courage of a great political strategist, and proudly confident in his hold upon the main body of his party, he prepared for both the attacks and the defections that were inevitable.

Defections, indeed, began at once. Even before the bill had been passed, the "Appeal of the Independent Democrats" was printed in a New York paper, with the signatures of members of Congress representing both the extreme anti-slavery wing of the Democrats and the organized Free-Soil party. The most famous of these names were those of Chase and Sumner, both of whom had been sent to the Senate by a coalition of Free-Soilers and Democrats. With them was the veteran abolitionist, Giddings of Ohio. The "Appeal" denounced Douglas as an "unscrupulous politician" and sounded both the warcries of the Northern masses by accusing him of being engaged in "an atrocious plot to exclude from a vast unoccupied region immigrants from the Old World and free laborers from our own States."

The events of the spring and summer of 1854 may all be grouped under two heads—the formation of an antiNebraska party, and the quick rush of sectional patriotism to seize the territory laid open by the Kansas-Nebraska Act. The instantaneous refusal of the Northerners to confine their settlement to Nebraska, and their prompt invasion of Kansas; the similar invasion from the South; the support of both movements by societies organized for that purpose; the war in Kansas all the details of this thrilling story have been told elsewhere.[2] The political story alone concerns us here.

When the fight began there were four parties in the field: the Democrats, the Whigs, the Free-Soilers, and the Know-Nothings.

The Free-Soil party, hitherto a small organization, had sought to make slavery the main issue in politics. Its watchword was "Free soil, free speech, free labor, and free men." It is needless to add that it was instantaneous in its opposition to the Kansas-Nebraska Act.

The Whigs at the moment enjoyed the greatest prestige, owing to the association with them of such distinguished leaders as Webster and Clay. In 1854, however, as a party they were dying, and the very condition that had made success possible for the Democrats made it impossible for the Whigs, because the latter stood for positive ideas, and aimed to be national in reality and not in the evasive Democratic sense of the term. For, as a

---

[2] See Jesse Macy, "The Anti-Slavery Crusade". (In "The Chronicles of America".)

matter of fact, on analysis all the greater issues of the day proved to be sectional. The Whigs would not, like the Democrats, adopt a negative attitude toward these issues, nor would they consent to become merely sectional. Yet at the moment negation and sectionalism were the only alternatives, and between these millstones the Whig organization was destined to be ground to bits and to disappear after the next Presidential election.

Even previous to 1854, numbers of Whigs had sought a desperate outlet for their desire to be positive in politics and had created a new party which during a few years was to seem a reality and then vanish together with its parent. The one chance for a party which had positive ideas and which wished not to be sectional was the definite abandonment of existing issues and the discovery of some new issue not connected with sectional feeling. Now, it happened that a variety of causes, social and religious, had brought about bad blood between native and foreigner, in some of the great cities, and upon the issue involved in this condition the failing spirit of the Whigs fastened. A secret society which had been formed to oppose the naturalization of foreigners quickly became a recognized political party. As the members of the Society answered all questions with "I do not know," they came to be called "Know-Nothings," though they called themselves "Americans." In those states where the Whigs had been strongest—Massachusetts, New York, and Pennsylvania—this last attempt to apply their former temper, though not their principles, had for a moment some success; but it could not escape the fierce division which was forced on the country by Douglas. As a result, it rapidly split into factions, one of which merged with the enemies of Douglas, while the other was lost among his supporters.

What would the great dying Whig party leave behind it? This was the really momentous question in 1854. Briefly, this party bequeathed the temper of political positivism and at the same time the dread of sectionalism. The inner clue to American politics during the next few years is, to many minds, to be found largely in the union of this old Whig temper with a new-born sectional patriotism, and, to other minds, in the gradual and reluctant passing of the Whig opposition to a sectional party. But though this transformation of the wrecks of Whiggism began immediately, and while the Kansas-Nebraska Bill was still being hotly debated in Congress, it was not until 1860 that it was completed.

In the meantime various incidents had shown that the sectional patriotism of the North, the fury of the abolitionists, and the positive temper in politics, were all drawing closer together. Each of these tendencies can be briefly illustrated. For example, the rush to Kansas had begun, and the Massachusetts Emigrant Aid Society was preparing to assist settlers who were going west. In May, there occurred at Boston one of the most conspicuous attempts to rescue a fugitive slave, in which a mob led by Thomas Wentworth Higginson attacked the guards of Anthony Burns, a captured fugitive, killed one of them, but failed to get the slave, who was carried to a revenue cutter between lines of soldiers and returned to slavery. Among numerous details of the hour the burning of Douglas in effigy is perhaps worth passing notice. In duly the anti-Nebraska men of Michigan held a convention, at which they organized as a political party and nominated a state ticket. Of their nominees, two had hitherto ranked themselves as Free-Soilers, three as anti-slavery Democrats, and five as Whigs. For the name of their party they chose "Republican," and as the foundation of their platform the resolution "That, postponing and suspending all differences with regard to political economy or administrative policy," they would "act cordially and faithfully in unison," opposing the extension of slavery, and would "cooperate and be known as 'Republicans' until the contest be terminated."

The history of the next two years is, in its main outlines, the story of the war in Kansas and of the spread of this new party throughout the North. It was only by degrees, however, that the Republicans absorbed the various groups of anti-Nebraska men. What happened at this time in Illinois may be taken as typical, and it is particularly noteworthy as revealing the first real appearance of Abraham Lincoln in American history.

Though in 1854 he was not yet a national figure, Lincoln was locally accredited with keen political insight, and was, regarded in Illinois as a strong lawyer. The story is told of him that, while he was attending court on the circuit, he heard the news of the Kansas-Nebraska Act in a tavern and sat up most of the night talking about it. Next morning he used a phrase destined to become famous. "I tell you," said he to a fellow lawyer, "this nation cannot exist half slave and half free."

Lincoln, however, was not one of the first to join the Republicans. In Illinois, in 1854, Lincoln resigned his seat in the legislature to become the Whig candidate for United States senator, to succeed the Democratic colleague of Douglas. But there was little chance of his election, for the real contest was between the two wings of the Democrats, the Nebraska men and the anti-Nebraska men, and Lincoln withdrew in favor of the candidate of the latter, who was elected.

During the following year, from the midst of his busy law practice, Lincoln watched the Whig party go to pieces. He saw a great part of its vote lodge temporarily among the Know-Nothings, but before the end of the year even they began to lose their prominence. In the autumn, from the obscurity of his provincial life, he saw, far off, Seward, the most astute politician of the day, join the new movement. In New York, the Republican state convention and the Whig state convention merged into one, and Seward pronounced a baptismal oration upon the Republican party of New York.

In the House of Representatives which met in December, 1855, the anti-Nebraska men were divided among themselves, and the Know-Nothings held the balance of power. No candidate for the speakership, however, was able to command a majority, and finally, after it had been agreed that a plurality would be sufficient, the contest closed, on the one hundred and thirty-third ballot, with the election of a Republican, N. P. Banks. Meanwhile in the South, the Whigs were rapidly leaving the party, pausing a moment with the Know-Nothings, only to find that their inevitable resting-place, under stress of sectional feeling, was with the Democrats.

On Washington's birthday, 1856, the Know-Nothing national convention met at Philadelphia. It promptly split upon the subject of slavery, and a portion of its membership sent word offering support to another convention which was sitting at Pittsburgh, and which had been called to form a national organization for the Republican party. A third assembly held on this same day was composed of the newspaper editors of Illinois, and may be looked upon as the organization of the Republican party in that state. At the dinner following this informal convention, Lincoln, who was one of the speakers, was toasted as "the next United States Senator."

Some four months afterward, in Philadelphia, the Republicans held their first national convention. Only a few years previous its members had called themselves by various names—Democrats, Free-Soilers, Know-Nothings, Whigs. The old hostilities of these different groups had not yet died out. Consequently, though Seward was far and away the most eminent member of the new party, he was not nominated for President. That dangerous honor was bestowed upon a dashing soldier and explorer of the Rocky Mountains and the Far West, John C. Fremont.[3]

The key to the political situation in the North, during that momentous year, was to be found in the great number of able Whigs who, seeing that their own party was lost but refusing to be sidetracked by the make-believe issue of the Know-Nothings, were now hesitating what to do. Though the ordinary politicians among the Republicans doubtless wished to conciliate these unattached Whigs, the astuteness of the leaders was too great to allow them to succumb to that temptation. They seem to have feared the possible effect of immediately incorporating in their ranks, while their new organization was still so plastic, the bulk of those conservative classes which were, after all, the backbone of this irreducible Whig minimum.

The Republican campaign was conducted with a degree of passion that had scarcely been equaled in America before that day. To the well-ordered spirit of the conservative classes the tone which the Republicans assumed appeared shocking. Boldly sectional in their language, sweeping in their denunciation of slavery, the leaders of the campaign made bitter and effective use of a number of recent events. "Uncle Tom's Cabin", published in 1852, and already immensely popular, was used as a political tract to arouse, by its gruesome picture of slavery, a hatred of slaveholders. Returned settlers from Kansas went about the North telling horrible stories of guerrilla warfare, so colored as to throw the odium all on one side. The scandal of the moment was the attack made by Preston Brooks on Sumner, after the latter's furious diatribe in the Senate, which was published as "The Crime Against Kansas". With double skill the Republicans made equal capital out of the intellectual violence of the speech and the physical violence of the retort. In addition to this, there was ready to their hands the evidence of Southern and Democratic sympathy with a filibustering attempt to conquer the republic of Nicaragua, where William Walker, an American adventurer, had recently made himself dictator. Walker had succeeded in having his minister acknowledged by the Democratic Administration, and in obtaining the endorsement of a great Democratic meeting which was held in New York. It looked, therefore, as if the party of political evasion had an anchor to windward,

---

[3] For an account of Fremont, see Stewart Edward White, "The Forty-Niners" (in "The Chronicles of America"), Chapter II.

and that, in the event of their losing in Kansas, they intended to placate their Southern wing by the annexation of Nicaragua.

Here, indeed, was a stronger political tempest than Douglas, weatherwise though he was, had foreseen. How was political evasion to brave it? With a courage quite equal to the boldness of the Republicans, the Democrats took another tack and steered for less troubled waters. Their convention at Cincinnati was temperate and discreet in all its expressions, and for President it nominated a Northerner, James Buchanan of Pennsylvania, a man who was wholly dissociated in the public mind from the struggle over Kansas.

The Democratic party leaders knew that they already had two strong groups of supporters. Whatever they did, the South would have to go along with them, in its reaction against the furious sectionalism of the Republicans. Besides the Southern support, the Democrats counted upon the aid of the professional politicians—those men who considered politics rather as a fascinating game than as serious and difficult work based upon principle. Upon these the Democrats could confidently rely, for they already had, in Douglas in the North and Toombs in the South, two master politicians who knew this type and its impulses intimately, because they themselves belonged to it. But the Democrats needed the support of a third group. If they could only win over the Northern remnant of the Whigs that was still unattached, their position would be secure. In their efforts to obtain this additional and very necessary reinforcement, they decided to appear as temperate and restrained as possible—a well bred party which all mild and conservative men could trust.

This attitude they formulated in connection with Kansas, which at that time had two governments: one, a territorial government, set up by emigrants from the South; the other, a state government, under the constitution drawn up at Topeka by emigrants from the North. One authorized slavery; the other prohibited slavery; and both had appealed to Washington for recognition. It was with this quite definite issue that Congress was chiefly concerned in the spring of 1856. During the summer Toombs introduced a bill securing to the settlers of Kansas complete freedom of action and providing for an election of delegates to a convention to draw up a state constitution which would determine whether slavery or freedom was to prevail—in other words, whether Kansas was to be annexed to the South or to the North. This bill was merely the full expression of what Douglas had aimed at in 1854 and of what was nicknamed "popular sovereignty"—the right of the locality to choose for itself between slave and free labor.

Two years before, such a measure would have seemed radical. But in politics time is wonderfully elastic. Those two years had been packed with turmoil. Kansas had been the scene of a bloody conflict. Regardless of which side had a majority on the ground, extremists on each side had demanded recognition for the government set up by their own party. By contrast, Toombs's offer to let the majority rule appeared temperate.

The Republicans saw instantly that they must discredit the proposal or the ground would be cut from under them. Though the bill passed the Senate, they were able to set it aside in the House in favor of a bill admitting Kansas as a free state with the Topeka constitution. The Democrats thereupon accused the Republicans of not wanting peace and of wishing to keep up the war-cry "Bleeding Kansas" until election time.

That, throughout the country, the two parties continued on the lines of policy they had chosen may be seen from an illustration. A House committee which had gone to Kansas to investigate submitted two reports, one of which, submitted by a Democratic member, told the true story of the murders committed by John Brown at Pottawatomie. And yet, while the Republicans spread everywhere their shocking tales of murders of free-state settlers, the Democrats made practically no use of this equally shocking tale of the murder of slaveholders. Apparently they were resolved to appear temperate and conservative to the bitter end.

And they had their reward. Or, perhaps the fury of the Republicans had its just deserts. From either point of view, the result was a choice of evils on the part of the reluctant Whigs, and that choice was expressed in the following words by as typical a New Englander as Rufus Choate: "The first duty of Whigs," wrote Choate to the Maine State central committee, "is to unite with some organization of our countrymen to defeat and dissolve the new geographical party calling itself Republican . . . The question for each and every one of us is . . . by what vote can I do most to prevent the madness of the times from working its maddest act the very ecstasy of its madness—the permanent formation and the actual triumph of a party which knows one half of America only to hate and dread it. If the Republican party," Choate continued, "accomplishes its object and gives the government to the North, I turn my eyes from the consequences. To the fifteen states of the South that government will appear an alien government. It will appear worse. It will appear a hostile government. It will represent to their eye a vast region of states organized upon anti-slavery, flushed by triumph, cheered onward by the voice of the pulpit, tribune, and press; its mission, to inaugurate freedom and put down the oligarchy; its constitution, the glittering and sounding generalities of natural right which make up the Declaration of Independence . . . Practically the contest, in my judgment, is between Mr. Buchanan and Colonel Fremont. In these circumstances, I vote for Mr. Buchanan."

The party of political evasion thus became the refuge of the old original Whigs who were forced to take advantage of any port in a storm. Buchanan was elected by an overwhelming majority. To the careless eye, Douglas had been justified by results; his party had triumphed as perhaps never before; and yet, no great political success was ever based upon less stable foundations. To maintain this position, those Northerners who reasoned as Choate did were a necessity; but to keep them in the party of political evasion would depend upon the ability of this party to play the game of politics without acknowledging sectional bias. Whether this difficult task could be accomplished would depend upon the South. Toombs, on his part, was anxious to continue making the party of evasion play the great American game of politics, and in his eagerness he perhaps overestimated his hold upon the South. This, however, remains to be seen.

Already another faction had formed around William L. Yancey of Alabama—a faction as intolerant of political evasion as the Republicans themselves, and one that was eager to match the sectional Northern party by a sectional Southern party. It had for the moment fallen into line with the Toombs faction because, like the Whigs, it had not the courage to do otherwise. The question now was whether it would continue fearful, and whether political evasion would continue to reign.

The key to the history of the next four years is in the growth of this positive Southern party, which had the inevitable result of forcing the Whig remainder to choose, not as in 1856 between a positive sectional policy and an evasive nonsectional policy, but in 1860 between two policies both of which were at once positive and sectional.

CHAPTER III.
THE POLITICIANS AND THE NEW DAY

The South had thus far been kept in line with the cause of political evasion by a small group of able politicians, chief among whom were Robert Toombs, Howell Cobb, and Alexander H. Stephens. Curiously enough all three were Georgians, and this might indeed be called the day of Georgia in the history of the South.

A different type of man, however, and one significant of a divergent point of view, had long endeavored to shake the leadership of the Georgian group. Rhett in South Carolina, Jefferson Davis in Mississippi, and above all Yancey in Alabama, together with the interests and sentiment which they represented, were almost ready to contest the orthodoxy of the policy of "nothing doing." To consolidate the interests behind them, to arouse and fire the sentiment on which they relied, was now the confessed purpose of these determined men. So little attention has hitherto been given to motive in American politics that the modern student still lacks a clear-cut and intelligent perception of these various factions. In spite of this fact, however, these men may safely be regarded as being distinctly more intellectual, and as having distinctly deeper natures, than the men who came together under the leadership of Toombs and Cobb, and who had the true provincial enthusiasm for politics as the great American sport.

The factions of both Toombs and Yancey were intensely Southern and, whenever a crisis might come, neither meant to hesitate an instant over striking hard for the South. Toombs, however, wanted to prevent such a situation, while Yancey was anxious to force one. The former conceived felicity as the joy of playing politics on the biggest stage, and he therefore bent all his strength to preserving the so-called national parties; the latter, scornful of all such union, was for a separate Southern community.

Furthermore, no man could become enthusiastic about political evasion unless by nature he also took kindly to compromise. So, Toombs and his followers were for preserving the negative Democratic position of 1856. In a formal paper of great ability Stephens defended that position when he appeared for reelection to Congress in 1857. Cobb, who had entered Buchanan's Cabinet as Secretary of the Treasury, and who spoke hopefully of making Kansas a slave state, insisted nevertheless that such a change must be "brought about by the recognized principles of carrying out the will of the majority which is the great doctrine of the Kansas Bill." To Yancey, as to the Republicans, Kansas was a disputed border-land for which the so-called two nations were fighting.

The internal Southern conflict between these two factions began anew with the Congressional elections of 1857. It is worth observing that the make-up of these factions was almost a resurrection of the two groups which, in 1850, had divided the South on the question of rejecting the Compromise. In a letter to Stephens in reference to one of the Yancey men, Cobb prophesied: "McDonald will utterly fail to get up a new Southern Rights party. Burnt children dread the fire, and he cannot get up as strong an organization as he did in 1850. Still it is necessary to guard every point, as McDonald is a hard hand to deal with." For the moment, he foretold events correctly. The Southern elections of 1857 did not break the hold of the moderates.

Yancey turned to different machinery, quite as useful for his purpose. This he found in the Southern commercial conventions, which were held annually. At this point there arises a vexed question which has, of late, aroused much discussion. Was there then what we should call today a slave "interest"? Was organized capital deliberately exploiting slavery? And did Yancey play into its hands?[4] The truth seems to be that, between 1856 and 1860, both the idealist parties, the Republicans and the

---

[4] For those who would be persuaded that there was such a slave interest, perhaps the best presentation is to be found in Professor Dodd's Life of Jefferson Davis.

Secessionists, made peace with, shall we say, the Mammon of unrighteousness, or merely organized capital? The one joined hands with the iron interest of the North; the other, with the slave interest of the South. The Republicans preached the domination of the North and a protective tariff; the Yancey men preached the independence of the South and the reopening of the slave trade.

These two issues Yancey, however, failed to unite, though the commercial convention of 1859 at last gave its support to a resolution that all laws, state or federal, prohibiting the African slave trade ought to be repealed. That great body of Northern capital which had dealings with the South was ready, as it always had been, to finance any scheme that Southern business desired. Slavers were fitted out in New York, and the city authorities did not prevent their sailing. Against this somber background stands forth that much admired action of Lewis Cass of Michigan, Buchanan's Secretary of State. Already the slave trade was in process of revival, and the British Navy, impelled by the powerful anti-slavery sentiment in England, was active in its suppression. American ships suspected of being slavers were visited and searched. Cass seized his opportunity, and declaring that such things "could not be submitted to by an independent nation without dishonor," sent out American warships to prevent this interference. Thereupon the British government consented to give up trying to police the ocean against slavers. It is indeed true, therefore, that neither North nor South has an historical monopoly of the support of slavery!

It is but fair to add that, so far as the movement to reopen the slave trade found favor outside the slave barons and their New York allies, it was advocated as a means of political defense, of increasing Southern population as an offset to the movement of free emigration into the North, and of keeping the proportion of Southern representation in Congress. Stephens, just after Cass had successfully twisted the lion's tail, took this position in a speech that caused a sensation. In a private letter he added, "Unless we get immigration from abroad, we shall have few more slave states. This great truth seems to take the people by surprise. Some shrink from it as they would from death. Still, it is as true as death." The scheme, however, never received general acceptance; and in the constitution of the Southern Confederacy there was a section prohibiting the African slave trade. On the other of these two issues—the independence of the South—Yancey steadily gained ground. With each year from 1856 to 1860, a larger proportion of Southerners drew out of political evasion and gave adherence to the idea of presenting an ultimatum to the North, with secession as an alternative.

Meanwhile, Buchanan sent to Kansas, as Governor, Robert J. Walker, one of the most astute of the Democrats of the opposite faction and a Mississippian. The tangled situation which Walker found, the details of his attempt to straighten it out, belong in another volume.[5] It is enough in this connection merely to mention the episode of the Lecompton convention in the election of which the Northern settlers refused to participate, though Walker had promised that they should have full protection and a fair count as well as that the work of the convention should be submitted to a popular vote. This action of Walker's was one more cause of contention between the warring factions in the South. The fact that he had met the Northerners half-way was seized upon by the Yancey men as evidence of the betrayal of the South by the Democratic moderates. On the other hand, Cobb, writing of the situation in Kansas, said that "a large majority are against slavery and ... our friends regard the fate of Kansas as a free state pretty well fixed . . . the pro-slavery men, finding that Kansas was likely to become a Black Republican State, determined to unite with the free-state Democrats." Here is the clue to Walker's course. As a strict party man, he preferred to accept Kansas free, with Democrats in control, rather than risk losing it altogether.

The next step in the affair is one of the unsolved problems in American history. Buchanan suddenly changed front, disgraced Walker, and threw himself into the arms of the Southern extremists. Though his reasons for doing so have been debated to this day, they have not yet been established beyond dispute. What seems to be the favorite explanation is that Buchanan was in a panic. What brought him to that condition may have been the following events.

The free-state men, by refusing to take part in electing the convention, had given control to the slaveholders, who proved they were not slow to seize their opportunity. They drew up a constitution favoring slavery, but this constitution, Walker had promised, was to be submitted in referendum. If the convention decided, however, not to submit the constitution, would not Congress have the right to accept it and admit

---

[5] See Jesse Macy, "The Anti-Slavery Crusade". (In "The Chronicles of America".)

Kansas as a Mate? This question was immediately raised. It now became plain that, by refusing to take part in the election, the free-state Kansans had thrown away a great tactical advantage. Of this blunder in generalship the Yancey men took instant advantage. It was known that the proportion of Free-Soilers in Kansas was very great—perhaps a majority—and the Southerners reasoned that they should not be obliged to give up the advantage they had won merely to let their enemies retrieve their mistake. Jefferson Davis formulated this position in an address to the Mississippi Legislature in which he insisted that Congress, not the Kansas electorate, was entitled to create the Kansas constitution, that the Convention was a properly chosen body, and that its work should stand. What Davis said in a stately way, others said in a furious way. Buchanan stated afterward that he changed front because certain Southern States had threatened that, if he did not abandon Walker, they would secede.

Be that as it may, Buchanan did abandon Walker and threw all the influence of the Administration in favor of admitting Kansas with the Lecompton constitution. But would this be true to that principle of "popular sovereignty" which was the very essence of the Kansas-Nebraska Act? Would it be true to the principle that each locality should decide for itself between slavery and freedom? On this issue the Southerners were fairly generally agreed and maintained that there was no obligation to go behind the work of the convention. Not so, however, the great exponent of popular sovereignty, Douglas. Rising in his place in the Senate, he charged the President with conspiring to defeat the will of the majority in Kansas. "If Kansas wants a slave state constitution," said he, "she has a right to it; if she wants a free state constitution, she has a right to it. It is none of my business which way the slavery clause is decided. I care not whether it is voted up or down."

There followed one of those prolonged legislative battles for which the Congress of the United States is justly celebrated. Furious oratory, propositions, counter-propositions, projected compromises, other compromises, and at the end nothing positive. But Douglas had defeated the attempt to bring in Kansas with the Lecompton constitution. As to the details of the story, they include such distinguished happenings as a brawling, all-night session when "thirty men, at least, were engaged in the fisticuff," and one Representative knocked another down.

Douglas was again at the center of the stage, but his term as Senator was nearing its end. He and the President had split their party. Pursued by the vengeful malice of the Administration, Douglas went home in 1858 to Illinois to fight for his reelection. His issue, of course, was popular sovereignty. His temper was still the temper of political evasion. How to hold fast to his own doctrine, and at the same time keep to his programme of "nothing doing"; how to satisfy the negative Democrats of the North without losing his last hold on the positive men of the South—such were his problems, and they were made still more difficult by a recent decision of the Supreme Court.

The now famous case of Dred Scott had been decided in the previous year. Its bewildering legal technicalities may here be passed over; fundamentally, the real question involved was the status of a negro, Dred Scott. A slave who had been owned in Missouri, and who had been taken by his master to the State of Illinois, to the free territory of Minnesota, and then back to Missouri, now claimed to be free. The Supreme Court undertook to decide whether his residence in Minnesota rendered him free, and also whether any negro of slave descent could be a citizen of the United States. The official opinion of the Court, delivered by Chief Justice Taney, decided both questions against the suppliant. It was held that the "citizens" recognized by the Constitution did not include negroes. So, even if Scott were free, he could not be considered a citizen entitled to bring suit in the Federal Courts. Furthermore, he could not be considered free, in spite of his residence in Minnesota, because, as the Court now ruled, Congress, when it enacted the Missouri Compromise, had exceeded its authority; the enactment had never really been in force; there was no binding prohibition of slavery in the Northwestern territories.

If this decision was good law, all the discussion about popular sovereignty went for nothing, and neither an act of Congress nor the vote of the population of a territory, whether for or against slavery, was of any value whatsoever. Nothing mattered until the newmade state itself took action after its admission to the Union. Until that time, no power, national or local, could lawfully interfere with the introduction of slaves. In the case of Kansas, it was no longer of the least importance what became of the Lecompton constitution or of any other that the settlers might make. The territory was open to settlement by slaveholders and would continue to be so as long as it remained a territory. The same conditions existed in Nebraska and in all the Northwest. The Dred Scott decision was accepted as orthodox Democratic doctrine by the South, by the Administration, and by the "Northern men with Southern principles." The astute masters of the game of politics on the Democratic side struck the note of legality. This was law, the expression of the highest tribunal of the Republic; what more was to be said? Though in truth there was but one other thing to be said, and that revolutionary, the Republicans, nevertheless, did not falter over it. Seward announced it in a speech in Congress on "Freedom in Kansas," when he uttered this menace: "We shall reorganize the Court and thus reform its political sentiments and practices."

In the autumn of 1858 Douglas attempted to perform the acrobatic feat of reconciling the Dred Scott decision, which as a Democrat he had to accept, with that idea of popular sovereignty without which his immediate followers could not be content. In accepting the Republican nomination as Douglas's opponent for the senatorship, Lincoln used these words which have taken rank among his most famous utterances: "A house divided against itself cannot stand. I believe this government cannot endure permanently half slave and half free. I do not expect the Union to be dissolved. I do not expect the house to fall but I do expect it will cease to be divided. It will become all one thing or all the other. Either the opponents of slavery will arrest the further spread of it, and place it where the public mind shall rest in the belief that it is in the course of ultimate extinction; or its advocates will push it forward till it shall become alike lawful in all the states, old as well as new—North as well as South."

No one had ever so tellingly expressed the deathgrapple of the sections: slavery the weapon of one, free labor the weapon of the other. Though Lincoln was at that time forty-nine years old, his political experience, in contrast with that of Douglas, was negligible. He afterward aptly described his early life in that expressive line from Gray, "The short and simple annals of the poor." He lacked regular schooling, and it was altogether from the practice of law that he had gained such formal education as he had. In law, however, he had become a master, and his position, to judge from the class of cases entrusted to him, was second to none in Illinois. To that severe yet wholesome cast of mind which the law establishes in men naturally lofty, Lincoln added the tonic influence of a sense of style—not the verbal acrobatics of a rhetorician, but that power to make words and thought a unit which makes the artist of a man who has great ideas. How Lincoln came by this literary faculty is, indeed, as puzzling as how Burns came by it. But there it was, disciplined by the court room, made pungent by familiarity with plain people, stimulated by constant reading of Shakespeare, and chastened by study of the Bible.

It was arranged that Douglas and Lincoln should tour the State together in a series of joint debates. As a consequence there followed a most interesting opposition of methods in the use of words, a contest between the method formed in Congress at a time when Congress was a perfect rhetorical academy, and that method of using words which was based on an arduous study of Blackstone, Shakespeare, and Isaiah. Lincoln issued from the debates one of the chief intellectual leaders of America, and with a place in English literature; Douglas came out a Senator from Illinois.

But though Douglas kept his following together, and though Lincoln was voted down, to Lincoln belonged the real strategic victory. In order to save himself with his own people, Douglas had been forced to make admissions that ruined him with the South. Because of these admissions the breach in the party of political evasion became irreparable. It was in the debate at Freeport that Douglas's fate overtook him, for Lincoln put this question: "Can the people of a United States territory, in any lawful way, against the wish of any citizen of the United States, exclude slavery from its limits, prior to the formation of a state constitution?"

Douglas answered in his best style of political thunder. "It matters not," he said, "what way the Supreme Court may hereafter decide as to the abstract question whether slavery may or may not go into a territory under the Constitution; the people have the lawful means to introduce it or exclude it as they please, for the reason that slavery cannot exist a day or an hour anywhere unless it is supported by local police regulations. Those police regulations can only be established by the local legislatures; and if the people are opposed to slavery, they will elect representatives to that body who will by unfriendly legislation effectually prevent the introduction of it into their midst. If, on the contrary, they are for it, their legislation will favor its extension. Hence, no matter what the decision of the Supreme Court may be on that abstract question, still the right of the people to make a slave territory or a free territory is perfect and complete under the Nebraska Bill."

As to the moral aspect of his actions, Douglas must ultimately be judged by the significance which this position in which he placed himself assumed in his own mind. Friendly critics excuse him: an interpretation of the Dred Scott decision which explained it away as an irresponsible utterance on a subject outside the scope of the case, a mere obiter dictum, is the justification which is called in to save him from the charge of insincerity. His friends, today, admit that this interpretation was bad law, but maintain that it may have been good morals, and that Douglas honestly held it. But many of us have not yet advanced so far in critical generosity, and cannot help feeling that Douglas's position remains political legerdemain—an attempt by a great officer of the government, professing to defend the Supreme Court, to show the people how to go through the motions of obedience to the Court while defeating its intention. If not double-dealing in a strict sense, it must yet be considered as having in it the temper of double-dealing.[6] This was, indeed, the view of many men of his own day and, among them, of Lincoln. Yet the type of man on whom the masters of the game of politics relied saw nothing in Douglas's position at which to be disturbed. It was merely playing politics, and if that absorbing sport required one to carry water on both shoulders, why—play the game! Douglas was the man for people like that. They cheered him to the echo and sent him back to the Senate. So well was this type understood by some of Lincoln's friends that they had begged him, at least according to tradition, not to put the question at Freeport, as by doing so he would enable Douglas to save himself with his constituency. Lincoln saw further, however. He understood better than they the forces then at work in America. The reply reported of him was: "If Douglas answers, he can never be President, and the battle of 1860 is worth a hundred of this."

Well might Yancey and his followers receive with a shout of joy the "Freeport Doctrine," as Douglas's supreme evasion was called. Should Southerners trust any longer the man who had evolved from the principle of let-'em-alone to the principle of double-dealing? However, the Southerners were far from controlling the situation. Though the events of 1858 had created discord in the Democratic party, they had not consolidated the South. Men like Toombs and Stephens were still hopeful of keeping the States together in the old bond of political evasion. The Democratic machine, damaged though it was, had not yet lost its hold on the moderate South, and while that continued to be the case, there was still power in it.

---

[6] There are three ways of regarding Douglas's position: (1) As a daring piece of evasion designed to hold all the Democrats together; (2) as an attempt to secure his locality at all costs, taking his chances on the South; (3) as a sincere expression of the legal interpretation mentioned above. It is impossible in attempting to choose among these to escape wholly one's impression of the man's character.

CHAPTER IV.
THE CRISIS

The Southern moderates in 1859 form one of those political groups, numerous enough in history, who at a crisis arrest our imagination because of the irony of their situation. Unsuspecting, these men went their way, during the last summer of the old regime, busy with the ordinary affairs of state, absorbed in their opposition to the Southern radicals, never dreaming of the doom that was secretly moving toward them through the plans of John Brown. In the soft brilliancy of the Southern summer when the roses were in bloom, many grave gentlemen walked slowly up and down together under the oaks of their plantation avenues, in the grateful dusk, talking eagerly of how the scales trembled in Southern politics between Toombs and Yancey, and questioning whether the extremists could ride down the moderate South and reopen the slave trade. In all their wondering whether Douglas would ever come back to them or would prove the blind Samson pulling down their temple about their ears, there was never a word about the approaching shadow which was so much more real than the shades of the falling night, and yet so entirely shut away from their observation.

In this summer, Stephens withdrew as he thought from public life. With an intensely sensitive nature, he had at times flashes of strange feeling which an unsophisticated society would regard as prophetic inspirations. When he left Washington "on the beautiful morning of the 5th of March, 1859, he stood at the stern of the boat for some minutes gazing back at the capital." He had announced his intention of not standing again as a Representative, and one of his fellow-passengers asked jokingly whether he was thinking of his return as a Senator. Stephen's reply was full of emotion, "No, I never expect to see Washington again unless I am brought here as a prisoner of war." During the summer he endeavored to cast off his intuition of approaching disaster. At his plantation, "Liberty Hall," he endeavored to be content with the innumerable objects associated with his youth; he tried to feel again the grace of the days that were gone, the mysterious loveliness of the Southern landscape with its immense fields, its forests, its great empty spaces filled with glowing sunshine. He tried to possess his troubled soul with the severe intellectual ardor of the law. But his gift of second sight would not rest. He could not overcome his intuition that, for all the peace and dreaminess of the outward world, destiny was upon him. Looking out from his spiritual seclusion, he beheld what seemed to him complete political confusion, both local and national. His despairing mood found expression a little later in the words: "Indeed if we were now to have a Southern convention to determine upon the true policy of the South either in the Union or out of it, I should expect to see just as much profitless discussion, disagreement, crimination, and recrimination amongst the members of it from different states and from the same state, as we witness in the present House of Representatives between Democrats, Republicans, and Americans."

Among the sources of confusion Stephens saw, close at home, was the Southern battle over the reopening of the slave trade. The reality of that issue had been made plain in May, 1859, when the Southern commercial congress at Vicksburg entertained at the same time two resolutions: one, that the convention should urge all Southern States to amend their constitutions by a clause prohibiting the increase of African slavery; the other, that the convention urge all the Legislatures of Southern States to present memorials to Congress asking the repeal of the law against African slave trade. Of these opposed resolutions, the latter was adopted on the last day of the convention[7], though the moderates fought hard against it.

The split between Southern moderates and Southern radicals was

[7] It is significant that the composition of these Southern commercial congresses and the Congress of the whole Southern people was strikingly different in personnel. Very few members of the commercial congresses reappear in the Confederate Congress.

further indicated by their differing attitudes toward the adventurers from the United States in Central America. The Vicksburg Convention adopted resolutions which were thinly veiled endorsements of southward expansion. In the early autumn another Nicaraguan expedition was nipped in the bud by the vigilance of American naval forces. Cobb, prime factor in the group of Southern moderates as well as Secretary of the Treasury, wrote to Buchanan expressing his satisfaction at the event, mentioning the work of his own department in bringing it about, and also alluding to his arrangments to prevent slave trading off the Florida coast.

But the spirit of doubt was strong even among the moderates. Douglas was the target. Stephens gives a glimpse of it in a letter written during his last session in Congress. "Cobb called on me Saturday night," he writes. "He is exceedingly bitter against Douglas. I joked him a good deal, and told him he had better not fight, or he would certainly be whipped; that is, in driving Douglas out of the Democratic party. He said that if Douglas ever was restored to the confidence of the Democracy of Georgia, it would be over his dead body politically. This shows his excitement, that is all. I laughed at him, and told him he would run his feelings and his policy into the ground." The anger of Cobb, who was himself a confessed candidate for the Democratic nomination, was imperiling the Democratic national machine which Toombs was still struggling so resolutely to hold together. Indeed, as late as the autumn of 1859 the machine still held together.

Then came the man of destiny, the bolt from the blue, the end of the chapter. A marvelous fanatic—a sort of reincarnation of the grimmest of the Covenanters—by one daring act shattered the machine and made impossible any further coalition on the principle of "nothing doing." This man of destiny was John Brown, whose attack on Harper's Ferry took place October 16th, and whose execution by the authorities of Virginia on the charges of murder and treason occurred on the 2nd of December.

The incident filled the South with consternation. The prompt condemnation of it by many Republican leaders did not offset, in the minds of Southerners, the fury of praise accorded by others. The South had a ghastly tradition derived chiefly from what is known as Nat Turner's Rebellion in Virginia, a tradition of the massacre of white women and children by negroes. As Brown had set opt to rouse a slave rebellion, every Southerner familiar with his own traditions shuddered, identifying in imagination John Brown and Nat Turner. Horror became rage when the Southerners heard of enthusiastic applause in Boston and of Emerson's description of Brown as "that new saint" who was to "make the gallows glorious like the cross." In the excitement produced by remarks such as this, justice was not done to Lincoln's censure. In his speech at Cooper Institute in New York, in February, 1860, Lincoln had said: "John Brown's effort... in its philosophy corresponds with the many attempts related in history at the assassination of kings and emperors. An enthusiast broods over the oppression of a people, until he fancies himself commissioned by Heaven to liberate them. He ventures the attempt which ends in little else than in his own execution." A few months afterwards, the Republican national convention condemned the act of Brown as "among the gravest of crimes."

An immediate effect of the John Brown episode was a passionate outburst from all the radical press of the South in defense of slavery. The followers of Yancey made the most of their opportunity. The men who voted at Vicksburg to reopen the slave trade could find no words to measure their hatred of every one who, at this moment of crisis, would not declare slavery a blessing. Many of the men who opposed the slave traders also felt that, in the face of possible slave insurrection, the peril of their families was the one paramount consideration. Nevertheless, it is easy for the special pleader to give a wrong impression of the sentiment of the time. A grim desire for self-preservation took possession of the South, as well as a deadly fear of any person or any thing that tended directly or indirectly to incite the blacks to insurrection. Northerners of abolitionist sympathies were warned to leave the country, and in some cases they were tarred and feathered.

Great anger was aroused by the detection of book-agents who were distributing a furious polemic against slavery, "The Impending Crisis of the South: How to Meet It", by Hinton Rowan Helper, a Southerner of inferior social position belonging to the class known as poor whites. The book teemed with such sentences as this, addressing slaveholders: "Do you aspire to become victims of white non-slave-holding vengeance by day and of barbarous massacres by the negroes at night?" It is scarcely strange, therefore, that in 1859 no Southerner would hear a good word of anyone caught distributing the book. And yet, in the midst of all this vehement exaltation of slavery, the fight to prevent a reopening of the slave trade went bravely on. Stephens, writing to a friend who was correspondent for the "Southern Confederacy", in Atlanta, warned him in April, 1860, "neither to advocate disunion or the opening of the slave trade. The people here at present I believe are as much opposed to it as they are at the North; and I believe the Northern people could be induced to open it sooner than the Southern people."

The winter of 1859-1860 witnessed a famous congressional battle over the speakership. The new Congress which met in December contained 109 Republicans, 101 Democrats, and 27 Know-Nothings. The Republican candidate for speaker was John Sherman of Ohio. As the first ballot showed that he could not command a majority, a Democrat from Missouri introduced this resolution "Whereas certain members of this House, now in nomination for speaker, did endorse the book hereinafter mentioned, resolved, That the doctrines and sentiments of a certain book, called 'The Impending Crisis of the South: How to Meet It', are insurrectionary and hostile to the peace and tranquillity of the country, and that no member of this House, who has indorsed or recommended it, is fit to be speaker of the House."

During two months there were strange scenes in the House, while the clerk acted as temporary speaker and furious diatribes were thundered back and forth across the aisle that separated Republicans from Democrats, with a passage of fisticuffs or even a drawn pistol to add variety to the scene. The end of it all was a deal. Pennington, of the "People's Party" of New Jersey, who had supported Sherman but had not endorsed Helper, was given the Republican support; a Know-Nothing was made sergeant-at-arms; and Know-Nothing votes added to the Republican votes made Pennington speaker. In many Northern cities the news of his election was greeted with the great salute of a hundred guns, but at Richmond the papers came out in mourning type.

Two great figures now advanced to the center of the Congressional stage—Jefferson Davis, Senator from Mississippi, a lean eagle of a man with piercing blue eyes, and Judah P. Benjamin, Senator from Louisiana, whose perpetual smile cloaked an intellect that was nimble, keen, and ruthless. Both men were destined to play leading roles in the lofty drama of revolution; each was to experience a tragic ending of his political hope, one in exile, the other in a solitary proscription amid the ruins of the society for which he had sacrificed his all. These men, though often spoken of as mere mouthpieces of Yancey, were in reality quite different from him both in temper and in point of view.

Davis, who was destined eventually to become the target of Yancey's bitterest enmity, had refused ten years before to join in the secession movement which ignored Calhoun's doctrine that the South had become a social unit. Though a believer in slavery under the conditions of the moment, Davis had none of the passion of the slave baron for slavery at all costs. Furthermore, as events were destined to show in a startlingly dramatic way, he was careless of South Carolina's passion for state rights. He was a practical politician, but not at all the old type of the party of political evasion, the type of Toombs. No other man of the moment was on the whole so well able to combine the elements of Southern politics against those more negative elements of which Toombs was the symbol. The history of the Confederacy shows that the combination which Davis now effected was not as thorough as he supposed it was. But at the moment he appeared to succeed and seemed to give common purpose to the vast majority of the Southern people. With his ally Benjamin, he struck at the Toombs policy of a National Democratic party.

On the day following the election of Pennington, Davis introduced in the Senate a series of resolutions which were to serve as the Southern ultimatum, and which demanded of Congress the protection of slavery against territorial legislatures. This was but carrying to its logical conclusion that Dred Scott decision which Douglas and his followers proposed to accept. If Congress could not restrict slavery in the territories, how could its creature, a territorial legislature do so? And yet the Douglas men attempted to take away the power from Congress and to retain it for the territorial legislatures. Senator Pugh of Ohio had already locked horns with Davis on this point, and had attempted to show that a territorial Legislature was independent of Congress. "Then I would ask the Senator further," retorted the logical Davis, "why it is he makes an appropriation to pay members of the territorial legislature; how it is that he invests the Governor with veto power over their acts; and how it is that he appoints judges to decide upon the validity of their acts."

In the Democratic convention which met at Charleston in April, 1860, the waning power of political evasion made its last real stand against the rising power of political positivism. To accept Douglas and the idea that somehow territorial legislatures were free to do what Congress could not do, or to reject Douglas and endorse Davis's ultimatum—that in substance was the issue. "In this convention where there should be confidence and harmony," said the "Charleston Mercury", "it is plain that men feel as if they were going into a battle." In the committee on resolutions where the States were equally represented, the majority were anti-Douglas; they submitted a report affirming Davis's position that territorial legislatures had no right to prohibit slavery and that the Federal Government should protect slavery against them. The minority refused to go further than an approval of the Dred Scott case and a pledge to abide by all future decisions of the Supreme Court. After both reports had been submitted, there followed the central event of the convention—the now famous speech by Yancey which repudiated political evasion from top to bottom, frankly defended slavery, and demanded either complete guarantees for its continued existence or, as an alternative, Southern independence. Pugh instantly replied and summed up Yancey's speech as a demand upon Northern Democrats to say that slavery was right, and that it was their duty not only to let slavery alone but to aid in extending it. "Gentlemen of the South," he exclaimed, "you mistake us—you mistake us—we will not do it."

In the full convention, where the representation of the States was not equal, the Douglas men, after hot debate, forced the adoption of the minority report. Thereupon the Alabama delegation protested and formally withdrew from the convention, and other delegations followed. There was wild excitement in Charleston, where that evening in the streets Yancey addressed crowds that cheered for a Southern republic. The remaining history of the Democratic nominations is a matter of detail. The Charleston convention adjourned without making nominations. Each of its fragments reorganized as a separate convention, and ultimately two Democratic tickets were put into the field, with Breckinridge of Kentucky as the candidate on the Yancey ticket and Douglas on the other.

While the Democrats were thus making history through their fateful break-up into separate parties, a considerable number of the so-called best people of the country determined that they had nowhere politically to lay their heads. A few of the old Whigs were still unable to consort either with Republicans or with Democrats, old or new. The Know-Nothings, likewise, though their number had been steadily melting away, had not entirely disappeared. To unite these political remnants in any definite political whole seemed beyond human ingenuity. A common sentiment, however, they did have—a real love of the Union and a real unhappiness, because its existence appeared to be threatened. The outcome was that they organized the Constitutional Union Party, nominating for President John Bell of Tennessee, and for Vice President Edward Everett of Massachusetts. Their platform was little more than a profession of love of the Union and a condemnation of sectional selfishness.

This Bell and Everett ticket has a deeper significance than has generally been admitted. It reveals the fact that the sentiment of Union, in distinction from the belief in the Union, had become a real force in American life. There could be no clearer testimony to the strength of this feeling than this spectacle of a great congregation of moderate people, unable to agree upon anything except this sentiment, stepping between the sectional parties like a resolute wayfarer going forward into darkness along a perilous strand between two raging seas. That this feeling of Union was the same thing as the eager determination of the Republicans, in 1860, to control the Government is one of those historical fallacies that have had their day. The Republican party became, in time and under stress of war, the refuge of this sentiment and proved sufficiently far-sighted to merge its identity temporarily in the composite Union party of 1864. But in 1860 it was still a sectional party. Among its leaders Lincoln was perhaps the only Unionist in the same sense as Bell and Everett.

Perhaps the truest Unionists of the North, outside the Constitutional Union Party, in 1860, were those Democrats in the following of Douglas who, after fighting to the last ditch against both the sectional parties, were to accept, in 1861, the alternative of war rather than dissolution. The course of Douglas himself, as we shall see hereafter, showed that in his mind there was a fixed limit of concession beyond which he could not go. When circumstances forced him to that limit, the sentiment of Union took control of him, swept aside his political jugglery, abolished his time-serving, and drove him into cooperation with his bitterest foes that the Union might be saved. Nor was the pure sentiment of Union confined to the North and West. Though undoubtedly the sentiment of locality was more powerful through the South, yet when the test came in the election of 1860, the leading candidate of the upper South, in Virginia, Kentucky, and Tennessee, was John Bell, the Constitutional Unionist. In every Southern State this sentiment was able to command a considerable part of the vote.[8]

Widely different in temper were those stern and resolute men whose organization, in perfect fighting trim, faced eagerly the divided Democrats. The Republicans had no division among themselves upon doctrine. Such division as existed was due to the ordinary rivalry of

---

[8] A possible exception was South Carolina. As the presidential electors were appointed by the legislature, there is no certain record of minority sentiment.

political leaders. In the opinion of all his enemies and of most Americans, Seward was the Republican man of the hour. During much of 1859 he had discreetly withdrawn from the country and had left to his partisans the conduct of his campaign, which seems to have been going well when he returned in the midst of the turmoil following the death of John Brown. Nevertheless he was disturbed over his prospects, for he found that in many minds, both North and South, he was looked upon as the ultimate cause of all the turmoil. His famous speech on the "irrepressible conflict" was everywhere quoted as an exultant prophecy of these terrible latter days.

It was long the custom to deny to Seward any good motive in a speech which he now delivered, just as it was to deny Webster any good motive for his famous 7th of March speech. But such criticism is now less frequent than it used to be. Both men were seeking the Presidency; both, we may fairly believe, were shocked by the turmoil of political currents; each tried oiling the waters, and in the attempt each ruined his candidacy. Seward's speech in condemnation of John Brown in February, 1860, was an appeal to the conservative North against the radical North, and to many of his followers it seemed a change of front. It certainly gained him no new friends and it lost him some old ones, so that his star as a presidential candidate began its decline.

The first ballot in the Republican convention surprised the country. Of the votes, 233 were necessary for a choice. Seward had only 173 ½. Next to him, with 102 votes, stood none of the leading candidates, but the comparatively obscure Lincoln. A gap of more than 50 votes separated Lincoln from Cameron, Chase, and Bates. On the second ballot Seward gained 11 votes, while Lincoln gained 79. The enemies of Seward, finding it impossible to combine on any of the conspicuous candidates, were moving toward Lincoln, the man with fewest enemies. The third ballot gave Lincoln the nomination.

We have seen that one of the basal questions of the time was which new political group should absorb the Whig remainder. The Constitutional Union party aimed to accomplish this. The Republicans sought to out-maneuver them. They made their platform as temperate as they could and yet consistent with the maintenance of their opposition to Douglas and popular sovereignty; and they went no further in their anti-slavery demands than that the territories should be preserved for free labor.

Another basal question had been considered in the Republican platform. Where would Northern capital stand in the reorganization of parties? Was capital, like men, to become frankly sectional or would it remain impersonal, careless how nations rose or fell, so long as dividends continued? To some extent capital had given an answer. When, in the excitement following the John Brown incident, a Southern newspaper published a white list of New York merchants whose political views should commend them to Southerners, and a black list of those who were objectionable, many New Yorkers sought a place in the white list. Northern capital had done its part in financing the revived slave trade. August Belmont, the New York representative of the Rothschilds, was one of the close allies of Davis, Yancey, and Benjamin in their war upon Douglas. In a word, a great portion of Northern capital had its heart where its investments were—in the South. But there was other capital which obeyed the same law, and which had investments in the North; and with this capital the Republicans had been trafficking. They had succeeded in winning over the powerful manufacturing interests of Pennsylvania, the pivotal State that had elected Buchanan in 1856.

The steps by which the new party of enthusiasm made its deal with the body of capital which was not at one with Belmont and the Democrats are not essential to the present narrative. Two facts suffice. In 1857 a great collapse in American business—"the panic of fifty-seven"—led the commercial world to turn to the party in power for some scheme of redress. But their very principles, among which was non-intervention in business, made the Democrats feeble doctors for such a need, and they evaded the situation. The Republicans, with their insistence on positivism in government, had therefore an opportunity to make a new application of the doctrine of governmental aid to business. In the spring of 1860, the Republican House of Representatives passed the Morrill tariff bill, consideration of which was postponed by the Democratic Senate. But it served its purpose: it was a Republican manifesto. The Republicans felt that this bill, together with their party platform, gave the necessary guarantee to the Pennsylvania manufacturers, and they therefore entered the campaign confident they would carry Pennsylvania nor was their confidence misplaced.

The campaign was characterized by three things: by an ominous quiet coupled with great intensity of feeling; by the organization of huge party societies in military form—"Wide-awakes" for Lincoln, numbering 400,000, and "Minute Men" for Breckenridge, with a membership chiefly

Southern; and by the perfect frankness, in all parts of the South, of threats of secession in case the Republicans won.

In none of the States which eventually seceded were any votes cast for Lincoln, with the exception of a small number in Virginia. In almost all the other Southern States and in the slave-holding border States, all the other candidates made respectable showings. In Virginia, Tennessee, and Kentucky, Bell led. But everywhere else in the other slave-holding States Breckinridge led, excepting in Missouri where Douglas won by a few hundred. Every free State except New Jersey went for Lincoln. And yet he did not have a majority of the popular vote, which stood: Lincoln, 1,866,459; Douglas, 1,376,957; Breckinridge, 849,781; Bell, 588,879[9]. The majority against Lincoln was nearly a million. The distribution of the votes was such that Lincoln had in the Electoral College, 180 electors; Breckinridge, 72; Bell, 39; Douglas, 12. In neither House of Congress did the Republicans have a majority.

---

[9] The figures of the popular vote are variously given by different compilers. These are taken from Stanwood, "A History of the Presidency".

CHAPTER V.
SECESSION

In tracing American history from 1854 to 1860 we cannot fail to observe that it reduces itself chiefly to a problem in that science which politicians understand so well—applied psychology. Definite types of men moulded by the conditions of those days are the determining factors—not the slavery question in itself; not, primarily, economic forces; not a theory of government, nor a clash of theories; not any one thing; but the fluid, changeful forces of human nature, battling with circumstances and expressing themselves in the fashion of men's minds. To say this is to acknowledge the fatefulness of sheer feeling. Davis described the situation exactly when he said, in 1860, "A sectional hostility has been substituted for a general fraternity." To his own question, "Where is the remedy?" he gave the answer, "In the hearts of the people." There, after all, is the conclusion of the whole matter. The strife between North and South had ceased to be a thing of the head; it had become a thing of the heart. Granted the emotions of 1860, the way in which our country staggered into war has all the terrible fascination of a tragedy on the theme of fate.

That a secession movement would begin somewhere in the South before the end of 1860 was a foregone conclusion. South Carolina was the logical place, and in South Carolina the inevitable occurred. The presidential election was quickly followed by an election of delegates, on the 6th of December, to consider in convention the relations of the State with the Union. The arguments before the Convention were familiar and had been advocated since 1851. The leaders of the disunionists were the same who had led the unsuccessful movement of ten years before. The central figure was Rhett, who never for a moment had wavered. Consumed his life long by the one idea of the independence of South Carolina, that stern enthusiast pressed on to a triumphant conclusion. The powers which had defeated him in 1851 were now either silent or converted, so that there was practically no opposition. In a burst of passionate zeal the independence of South Carolina was proclaimed on December 20, 1860, by an ordinance of secession.

Simultaneously, by one of those dramatic coincidences which make history stranger than fiction, Lincoln took a step which supplemented this action and established its tragic significance. What that step was will appear in a moment.

Even before the secession began, various types of men in politics had begun to do each after his kind. Those whom destiny drove first into a corner were the lovers of political evasion. The issue was forced upon them by the instantaneous demand of the people of South Carolina for possession of forts in Charleston Harbor which were controlled by the Federal Government. Anticipating such a demand, Major Robert Anderson, the commandant at Charleston, had written to Buchanan on the 23d of November that "Fort Sumter and Castle Pinckney must be garrisoned immediately, if the Government determines to keep command of this harbor."

In the mind of every American of the party of political evasion, there now began a sad, internal conflict. Every one of them had to choose among three courses: to shut his eyes and to continue to wail that the function of government is to do nothing; to make an end of political evasion and to come out frankly in approval of the Southern position; or to break with his own record, to emerge from his evasions on the opposite side, and to confess himself first and before all a supporter of the Union. One or another of these three courses, sooner or later, every man of the President's following chose. We shall see presently the relative strength of the three groups into which that following broke and what strange courses sometimes tragic, sometimes comic—two of the three pursued. For the moment our concern is how the division manifested itself among the heads of the party at Washington.

The President took the first of the three courses. He held it with the nervous clutch of a weak nature until overmastered by two grim men who gradually hypnotized his will. The turning-point for Buchanan, and the last poor crisis in his inglorious career, came on Sunday, December 30th. Before that day arrived, his vacillation had moved his friends to pity and his enemies to scorn. One of his best friends wrote privately, "The President is pale with fear"; and the hostile point of view found expression in such comments as this, "Buchanan, it is said, divides his time between praying and crying. Such a perfect imbecile never held office before."

With the question what to do about the forts hanging over his bewildered soul, Buchanan sent a message to Congress on December 4, 1860, in which he sought to defend the traditional evasive policy of his party. He denied the constitutional right of secession, but he was also denied his own right to oppose such a course. Seward was not unfair to the mental caliber of the message when he wrote to his wife that Buchanan showed "conclusively that it is the duty of the President to execute the laws—unless somebody opposes him; and that no State has a right to go out of the Union unless it wants to."

This message of Buchanan's hastened the inevitable separation of the Democratic party into its elements. The ablest Southern member of the Cabinet, Cobb, resigned. He was too strong an intellect to continue the policy of "nothing doing" now that the crisis had come. He was too devoted a Southerner to come out of political evasion except on one side. On the day Cobb resigned the South Carolina Representatives called on Buchanan and asked him not to make any change in the disposition of troops at Charleston, and particularly not to strengthen Sumter, a fortress on an island in the midst of the harbor, without at least giving notice to the state authorities. What was said in this interview was not put in writing but was remembered afterward in different ways with unfortunate consequences.

Every action of Buchanan in this fateful month continued the disintegration of his following. Just as Cobb had to choose between his reasonings as a Democratic party man and his feelings as a Southerner, so the aged Cass, his Secretary of State, and an old personal friend, now felt constrained to choose between his Democratic reasoning and his Northern sympathies, and resigned from the Cabinet on the 11th of December. Buchanan then turned instinctively to the strongest natures that remained among his close associates. It is a compliment to the innate force of Jeremiah S. Black, the Attorney-General, that Buchanan advanced him to the post of Secretary of State and allowed him to name as his successor in the Attorney-Generalship Edwin M. Stanton. Both were tried Democrats of the old style, "let-'em-alone" sort; and both had supported the President in his Kansas policy. But each, like every other member of his party, was being forced by circumstances to make his choice among the three inevitable courses, and each chose the Northern side. At once the question of the moment was whether the new Secretary of State and his powerful henchmen would hypnotize the President.

For a couple of weeks the issue hung in the balance. Then there appeared at Washington commissioners from South Carolina "empowered to treat . . . for the delivery of forts . . . and other real estate" held by the Federal Government within their State. On the day following their arrival, Buchanan was informed by telegraph that Anderson had dismantled Fort Moultrie on the north side of the harbor, had spiked its guns, and had removed its garrison to the island fortress, Sumter, which was supposed to be far more defensible. At Charleston his action was interpreted as preparation for war; and all South Carolinians saw in it a violation of a pledge which they believed the President had given their congressmen, three weeks previous, in that talk which had not been written down. Greatly excited and fearful of designs against them, the South Carolina commissioners held two conferences with the President on the 27th and 28th of December. They believed that he had broken his word, and they told him so. Deeply agitated and refusing to admit that he had committed himself at the earlier conference, he said that Anderson had acted on his own responsibility, but he refused to order him back to the now ruined Fort Moultrie. One remark which he let fall has been remembered as evidence of his querulous state of mind: "You are pressing me too importunately" exclaimed the unhappy President; "you don't give me time to consider; you don't give me time to say my prayers; I always say my prayers when required to act upon any great state affair." One remembers Hampden "seeking the Lord" about ship money, and one realizes that the same act may have a vastly different significance in different temperaments.

Buchanan, however, was virtually ready to give way to the demand of the commissioners. He drew up a paper to that effect and showed it to the Cabinet. Then the turning-point came. In a painful interview, Black, long one of his most trusted friends, told him of his intention to resign, and that Stanton would go with him and probably also the Postmaster-General, Holt. The idea of losing the support of these strong personalities terrified Buchanan, who immediately fell into a panic. Handing Black the paper he had drawn up, Buchanan begged him to retain office and to alter the paper as he saw fit. To this Black agreed. The demand for the surrender of the forts was refused; Anderson was not ordered back to Moultrie; and for the brief remainder of Buchanan's administration Black acted as prime minister.

A very powerful section of the Northern democracy, well typified by their leaders at Washington, had thus emerged from political evasion on the Northern side. These men, known afterwards as War Democrats, combined with the Republicans to form the composite Union party which supported Lincoln. It is significant that Stanton eventually reappeared in the Cabinet as Lincoln's Secretary of War, and that along with him appeared another War Democrat, Gideon Welles, Lincoln's Secretary of the Navy. With them, at last, Douglas, the greatest of all the old Democrats of the North, took his position. What became of the other factions of the old Democratic party remains to be told.

While Buchanan, early in the month, was weeping over the pitilessness of fate, more practical Northerners were grappling with the question of what was to be done about the situation. In their thoughts they anticipated a later statesman and realized that they were confronted by a condition and not by a theory. Secession was at last a reality. Which course should they take?

What strikes us most forcibly, as we look back upon that day, is the widespread desire for peace. The abolitionists form a conspicuous example. Their watchword was "Let the erring sisters go in peace." Wendell Phillips, their most gifted orator, a master of spoken style at once simple and melodious, declaimed splendidly against war. Garrison, in "The Liberator", followed his example. Whittier put the same feeling into his verse:

They break the links of Union; shall we light The flames of hell to weld anew the chain On that red anvil where each blow is pain?

Horace Greeley said in an editorial in the "New York Tribune": "If the cotton states shall decide that they can do better out of the Union than in it, we shall insist on letting them go in peace. Whenever a considerable section of our Union shall deliberately resolve to go out, we shall resist all coercive measures designed to keep them in. We hope never to live in a republic where one section is pinned to the residue by bayonets."

The Democrats naturally clung to their traditions, and, even when they went over, as Black and Stanton did, to the Anti-Southern group, they still hoped that war would not be the result. Equally earnest against war were most of the Republicans, though a few, to be sure, were ready to swing the

"Northern hammer." Summer prophesied that slavery would "go down in blood." But the bulk of the Republicans were for a sectional compromise, and among them there was general approbation of a scheme which contemplated reviving the line of the Missouri Compromise, and thus frankly admitting the existence of two distinct sections, and guaranteeing to each the security of its own institutions. The greatest Republican boss of that day, Thurlow Weed, came out in defense of this plan.

No power was arrayed more zealously on the side of peace of any kind than the power of money. It was estimated that two hundred millions of dollars were owed by Southerners to Northerners. War, it was reasoned, would cause the cancellation of these obligations. To save their Southern accounts, the moneyed interests of the North joined the extremists of Abolition in pleading to let the erring sisters go in peace, if necessary, rather than provoke them to war and the confiscation of debts. It was the dread of such an outcome—which finally happened and ruined many Northern firms—that caused the stock-market in New York to go up and down with feverish uncertainty. Banks suspended payment in Washington, Baltimore, and Philadelphia. The one important and all-engrossing thing in the mind's eye of all the financial world at this moment was that specter of unpaid Southern accounts.

At this juncture, Senator Crittenden of Kentucky submitted to the Senate a plan which has been known ever since as the Crittenden Compromise. It was similar to Weed's plan, but it also provided that the division of the country on the Missouri Compromise line should be established by a constitutional amendment, which would thus forever solidify sectionalism. Those elements of the population generally called the conservative and the responsible were delighted. Edward Everett wrote to Crittenden, "I saw with great satisfaction your patriotic movement, and I wish from the bottom of my heart it might succeed"; and August Belmont in a letter to Crittenden spoke for the moneyed interest: "I have yet to meet the first Union-loving man, in or out of politics, who does not approve your compromise proposition . . . "

The Senate submitted the Compromise to a Committee of Thirteen. In this committee the Southern leaders, Toombs and Davis, were both willing to accept the Compromise, if a majority of the Republican members would agree. Indeed, if the Republicans would agree to it, there seemed no reason why a new understanding between the sections might not be reached, and no reason why sectionalism, if accepted as the basis of the government, might not solve the immediate problem and thus avert war.

In this crisis all eyes were turned to Seward, that conspicuous Republican who was generally looked upon as the real head of his party. And Seward, at that very moment, was debating whether to accept Lincoln's offer of the Secretaryship of State, for he considered it vital to have an understanding with Lincoln on the subject of the Compromise. He talked the matter over with Weed, and they decided that Weed should go to Springfield and come to terms with Lincoln. It was the interview between Weed and Lincoln held, it seems, on the very day on which the Ordinance of Secession was adopted—which gave to that day its double significance.

Lincoln refused point-blank to accept the compromise and he put his refusal in writing. The historic meaning of his refusal, and the significance of his determination not to solve the problem of the hour by accepting a dual system of government based on frankly sectional assumptions, were probably, in a measure, lost on both Weed and Seward. They had, however, no misunderstanding of its practical effect. This crude Western lawyer had certain ideas from which he would not budge, and the party would have to go along with him. Weed and Seward therefore promptly fell into line, and Seward accepted the Secretaryship and came out in opposition to the Compromise. Other Republicans with whom Lincoln had communicated by letter made known his views, and Greeley announced them in The Tribune. The outcome was the solid alignment of all the Republicans in Congress against the Compromise. As a result, this last attempt to reunite the sections came to nothing.

Not more than once or twice, if ever, in American history, has there been such an anxious New Year's Day as that which ushered in 1861. A few days before, a Republican Congressman had written to one of his constituents: "The heavens are indeed black and an awful storm is gathering . . . I see no way that either North or South can escape its fury." Events were indeed moving fast toward disaster. The garrison at Sumter was in need of supplies, and in the first week of the new year Buchanan attempted to relieve its wants. But a merchant vessel, the Star of the West, by which supplies were sent, was fired upon by the South Carolina authorities as it approached the harbor and was compelled to turn back. This incident caused the withdrawal from the Cabinet of the last opposition members—Thompson, of Mississippi, the Secretary of the Interior, and Thomas, of Maryland, the Secretary of the Treasury. In the course of the month five Southern States followed South Carolina out of the Union, and their Senators and Representatives resigned from the Congress of the United States.

The resignation of Jefferson Davis was communicated to the Senate in a speech of farewell which even now holds the imagination of the student, and which to the men of that day, with the Union crumbling around them, seemed one of the most mournful and dramatic of orations. Davis possessed a beautiful, melodious voice; he had a noble presence, tall, erect, spare, even ascetic, with a flashing blue eye. He was deeply moved by the occasion; his address was a requiem. That he withdrew in sorrow but with fixed determination, no one who listened to him could doubt. Early in February, the Southern Confederacy was formed with Davis as its provisional President. With the prophetic vision of a logical mind, he saw that war was inevitable, and he boldly proclaimed his vision. In various speeches on his way South, he had assured the Southern people that war was coming, and that it would be long and bloody.

The withdrawal of these Southern members threw the control of the House into the hands of the Republicans. Their realization of their power was expressed in two measures which also passed the Senate; Kansas was admitted—as a State with an anti-slavery constitution; and the Morrill tariff, which they had failed to pass the previous spring, now became law. Thus the Republicans began redeeming their pledges to the anti-slavery men on the one hand and to the commercial interest on the other. The time had now arrived for the Republican nominee to proceed from Springfield to Washington. The journey was circuitous in order to enable Lincoln to speak at a number of places. Never before, probably, had the Northern people felt such tense strain as at that moment; never had they looked to an incoming President with such anxious doubt. Would he prevent war? Or, if he could not do that, would he be able to extricate the country—Heaven alone knew how!—without a terrible ordeal? Since his election, Lincoln had remained quietly at Springfield. Though he had influenced events through letters to Congressmen, his one conspicuous action during that winter was the defeat of the Crittenden Compromise. The Southern President had called upon his people to put their house in order as preparation for war. What, now, had Lincoln to say to the people of the North?

The biographers of Lincoln have not satisfactorily revealed the state of his mind between election and inauguration. We may safely guess that his silence covered a great internal struggle. Except for his one action in defeating the Compromise, he had allowed events to drift; but by that one action he had taken upon himself the responsibility for the drift. Though the country at that time did not fully appreciate this aspect of the situation, who now can doubt that Lincoln did? His mind was always a lonely one. His very humor has in it, so often, the note of solitude, of one who is laughing to make the best of things, of one who is spiritually alone. During those months when the country drifted from its moorings, and when war was becoming steadily more probable, Lincoln, after the manner of the prophets, wrestled alone with the problems which he saw before him. From the little we know of his inward state, it is hard for us to conclude that he was happy. A story which is told by his former partner, Mr. Herndon, seems significant. As Lincoln was leaving his unpretentious law-office for the last time, he turned to Mr. Herndon and asked him not to take down their old sign. "Let it hang there undisturbed," said he. "Give our clients to understand that the election of a President makes no difference in the firm . . . If I live, I'm coming back some time, and then we'll go right on practising law as if nothing had happened."

How far removed from self-sufficiency was the man whose thoughts, on the eve of his elevation to the Presidency, lingered in a provincial law office, fondly insistent that only death should prevent his returning some time and resuming in those homely surroundings the life he had led previous to his greatness. In a mood of wistfulness and of intense preoccupation, he began his journey to Washington. It was not the mood from which to strike fire and kindle hope. To the anxious, listening country his speeches on the journey to Washington were disappointing. Perhaps his strangely sensitive mind felt too powerfully the fatefulness of the moment and reacted with a sort of lightness that did not really represent the real man. Be that as it may, he was never less convincing than at that time. Nor were people impressed by his bearing. Often he appeared awkward, too much in appearance the country lawyer. He acted as a man who was ill at ease and he spoke as a man who had nothing to say. Gloom darkened the North as a consequence of these unfortunate speeches, for they expressed an optimism which we cannot believe he really felt, and which hurt him in the estimation of the country. "There is no crisis but an artificial one," was one of his ill-timed assurances, and another, "There is nothing going wrong . . . There is nothing that really hurts any one." Of his supporters some were discouraged; others were exasperated; and an able but angry partisan even went so far as to write in a private letter, "Lincoln is a Simple Susan."

The fourth of March arrived, and with it the end of Lincoln's blundering. One good omen for the success of the new Administration was the presence of Douglas on the inaugural platform. He had accepted fate, deeply as it wounded him, and had come out of the shattered party of evasion on the side of his section. For the purpose of showing his support of the administration at this critical time, he had taken a place on the stand where Lincoln was to speak. By one of those curious little dramatic touches with which chance loves to embroider history, the presence of Douglas became a gracious detail in the memory of the day. Lincoln, worn and awkward, continued to hold his hat in his hand. Douglas, with the tact born of social experience, stepped forward and took it from him without—exposing Lincoln's embarrassment.

The inaugural address which Lincoln now pronounced had little similarity to those unfortunate utterances which he had made on the journey to Washington. The cloud that had been over him, whatever it was, had lifted. Lincoln was ready for his great labor. The inaugural contained three main propositions. Lincoln pledged himself not to interfere directly or indirectly with slavery in the States where it then existed; he promised to support the enforcement of the fugitive slave law; and he declared he would maintain the Union. "No State," said he, "upon its own mere motion can lawfully get out of the Union . . . To the extent of my ability I shall take care, as the Constitution itself expressly enjoins upon me, that the laws of the Union be faithfully executed in all the States . . . In doing this, there need be no bloodshed or violence; and there shall be none, unless it be forced upon the national authority. The power confided to me will be used to hold, occupy, and possess the property and places belonging to the government." Addressing the Southerners, he said: "In your hands, my dissatisfied fellow-countrymen, and not in mine, is the momentous issue of civil war. The Government will not assail you . . . We are not enemies but friends . . . The mystic cords of memory, stretching from every battlefield and patriot grave to every living heart and hearthstone, all over this broad land, will yet swell the chorus of the Union, when again touched, as surely they will be, by the better angels of our nature."

Gentle, as was the phrasing of the inaugural, it was perfectly firm, and it outlined a policy which the South would not accept, and which, in the opinion of the Southern leaders, brought them a step nearer war. Wall Street held the same belief, and as a consequence the price of stocks fell.

CHAPTER VI.
WAR

On the day following the inauguration, commissioners of the newly formed Confederacy appeared at Washington and applied to the Secretary of State for recognition as envoys of a foreign power. Seward refused them such recognition. But he entered into a private negotiation with them which is nearly, if not quite, the strangest thing in our history. Virtually, Seward intrigued against Lincoln for control of the Administration. The events of the next five weeks have an importance out of all proportion to the brevity of the time. This was Lincoln's period of final probation. The psychological intensity of this episode grew from the consciousness in every mind that now, irretrievably, destiny was to be determined. War or peace, happiness or adversity, one nation or two—all these were in the balance. Lincoln entered the episode a doubtful quantity, not with certainty the master even in his own Cabinet. He emerged dominating the situation, but committed to the terrible course of war.

One cannot enter upon this great episode, truly the turning point in American history, without pausing for a glance at the character of Seward. The subject is elusive. His ablest biographer[10] plainly is so constantly on guard not to appear an apologist that he ends by reducing his portrait to a mere outline, wavering across a background of political details. The most

---

[10] Frederic Bancroft, "Life of William H. Seward".

recent study of Seward[11] surely reveals between the lines the doubtfulness of the author about pushing his points home. The different sides of the man are hard to reconcile. Now he seemed frank and honest; again subtle and insincere. As an active politician in the narrow sense, he should have been sagacious and astute, yet he displayed at the crisis of his life the most absolute fatuity. At times he had a buoyant and puerile way of disregarding fact and enveloping himself in a world of his own imagining. He could bluster, when he wished, like any demagogue; and yet he could be persuasive, agreeable, and even personally charming.

But of one thing with regard to Seward, in the first week of March, 1861, there can be no doubt: he thought himself a great statesman—and he thought Lincoln "a Simple Susan." He conceived his role in the new administration to involve a subtle and patient manipulation of his childlike superior. That Lincoln would gradually yield to his spell and insensibly become his figurehead; that he, Seward, could save the country and would go down to history a statesman above compare, he took for granted. Nor can he fairly be called conceited, either; that is part of his singularity.

Lincoln's Cabinet was, as Seward said, a compound body. With a view to strengthening his position, Lincoln had appointed to cabinet positions all his former rivals for the Republican nomination. Besides Seward, there was Chase as Secretary of the Treasury; Simon Cameron of Pennsylvania as Secretary of War; Edward Bates of Missouri as Attorney-General. The appointment of Montgomery Blair of Maryland as Postmaster-General was intended to placate the border Slave States. The same motive dictated the later inclusion of James Speed of Kentucky in the Cabinet. The Black-Stanton wing of the Democrats was represented in the Navy Department by Gideon Welles, and in course of time in the War Department also, when Cameron resigned and Stanton succeeded him. The West of that day was represented by Caleb B. Smith of Indiana.

Seward disapproved of the composition of the Cabinet so much that, almost at the last moment, he withdrew his acceptance of the State Department. It was Lincoln's gentleness of argument which overcame his reluctance to serve. We may be sure, however, that Seward failed to observe that Lincoln's tactlessness in social matters did not extend to his

---

[11] Gamaliel Bradford, "Union Portraits".

management of men in politics; we may feel sure that what remained in his mind was Lincoln's unwillingness to enter office without William Henry Seward as Secretary of State.

The promptness with which Seward assumed the role of prime minister bears out this inference. The same fact also reveals a puzzling detail of Seward's character which amounted to obtuseness—his forgetfulness that appointment to cabinet offices had not transformed his old political rivals Chase and Cameron, nor softened the feelings of an inveterate political enemy, Welles, the Secretary of the Navy. The impression which Seward made on his colleagues in the first days of the new Government has been thus sharply recorded by Welles: "The Secretary of State was, of course, apprised of every meeting [of ministers] and never failed in his attendance, whatever was the subject-matter, and though entirely out of his official province. He was vigilantly attentive to every measure and movement in other Departments, however trivial—as much so as to his own—watched and scrutinized every appointment that was made, or proposed to be made, but was not communicative in regard to the transaction of the State Department." So eager was Seward to keep all the threads of affairs in his own hands that he tried to persuade Lincoln not to hold cabinet meetings but merely to consult with particular ministers, and with the Secretary of State, as occasion might demand. A combined protest from the other Secretaries, however, caused the regular holding of Cabinet meetings.

With regard to the Confederacy, Seward's policy was one of non-resistance. For this he had two reasons. The first of these was his rooted delusion that the bulk of the Southerners were opposed to secession and, if let alone, would force their leaders to reconsider their action. He might have quoted the nursery rhyme, "Let them alone and they'll come home"; it would have been like him and in tune with a frivolous side of his nature. He was quite as irresponsible when he complacently assured the North that the trouble would all blow over within ninety days. He also believed that any display of force would convert these hypothetical Unionists of the South from friends to enemies and would consolidate opinion in the Confederacy to produce war. In justice to Seward it must be remembered that on this point time justified his fears.

His dealings with the Confederate commissioners show that he was playing to gain time, not with intent to deceive the Southerners but to acquire that domination over Lincoln which he felt was his by natural right. Intending to institute a peace policy the moment he gained this ascendency, he felt perfectly safe in making promises to the commissioners through mutual friends. He virtually told them that Sumter would eventually be given up and that all they need do was to wait.

Seward brought to bear upon the President the opinions of various military men who thought the time had passed when any expedition for the relief of Sumter could succeed. For some time Lincoln seemed about to consent, though reluctantly, to Seward's lead in the matter of the forts. He was pulled up standing, however, by the threatened resignation of the Postmaster-General, Blair. After a conference with leading Republican politicians the President announced to his Cabinet that his policy would include the relief of Sumter. "Seward," says Welles, " . . . was evidently displeased."

Seward now took a new tack. Fort Pickens, at Pensacola, was a problem similar to that of Sumter at Charleston. Both were demanded by the Confederates, and both were in need of supplies. But Fort Pickens lay to one side, so to speak, of the public mind, and there was not conspicuously in the world's eye the square issue over it that there was over Sumter. Seward conceived the idea that, if the President's attention were diverted from Sumter to Pickens and a relief expedition were sent to the latter but none to the former, his private negotiations with the Confederates might still be kept going; Lincoln might yet be hypnotized; and at last all would be well.

On All-Fools' Day, 1861, in the midst of a press of business, he obtained Lincoln's signature to some dispatches, which Lincoln, it seems, discussed with him hurriedly and without detailed consideration. There were now in preparation two relief expeditions, one to carry supplies to Pensacola, the other to Charleston. Neither was to fight if it was not molested. Both were to be strong enough to fight if their commanders deemed it necessary. As flagship of the Charleston expedition, Welles had detailed the powerful warship Powhatan, which was rapidly being made ready at the Brooklyn Navy Yard. Such was the situation as Welles understood it when he was thinking of bed late on the night of the 6th of April. Until then he had not suspected that there was doubt and bewilderment about the Powhatan at Brooklyn. One of those dispatches which Lincoln had so hastily signed provided for detaching the Powhatan from the Charleston expedition and sending it safe out of harm's way to Pensacola. The commander of the ship had before him the conflicting orders, one from the President, one from the Secretary of the Navy. He was about to sail under the President's orders for Pensacola; but wishing to make sure of his authority, he had telegraphed to Washington. Gideon Welles was a pugnacious man. His dislike for Seward was deepseated. Imagine his state of mind when it was accidently revealed to him that Seward had gone behind his back and had issued to naval officers orders which were contradictory to his own! The immediate result was an interview that same night between Seward and Welles in which, as Welles coldly admitted in after days, the Secretary of the Navy showed "some excitement." Together they went, about midnight, to the White House. Lincoln had some difficulty recalling the incident of the dispatch on the 1st of April; but when he did remember, he took the responsibility entirely upon himself, saying he had had no purpose but to strengthen the Pickens expedition, and no thought of weakening the expedition to Charleston. He directed Seward to telegraph immediately cancelling the order detaching the Powhatan. Seward made a desperate attempt to put him off, protesting, it was too late to send a telegram that night. "But the President was imperative," writes Secretary Welles, in describing the incident, and a dispatch was sent.

Seward then, doubtless in his agitation, did a strange thing. Instead of telegraphing in the President's name, the dispatch which he sent read merely, "Give up the Powhatan . . . Seward." When this dispatch was received at Brooklyn, the Powhatan was already under way and had to be overtaken by a fast tug. In the eyes of her commander, however, a personal telegram from the Secretary of State appeared as of no weight against the official orders of the President, and he continued his voyage to Pensacola.

The mercurial temper of Seward comes out even in the caustic narrative written afterwards by Welles. Evidently Seward was deeply mortified and depressed by the incident. He remarked, says Welles, that old as he was he had learned a lesson, and that was that he had better attend to his own business. "To this," commented his enemy, "I cordially assented."

Nevertheless Seward's loss of faith in himself was only momentary. A night's sleep was sufficient to restore it. His next communication to the commissioners shows that he was himself again, sure that destiny owed him the control of the situation. On the following day the commissioners had got wind of the relief expedition and pressed him for information, recalling his assurance that nothing would be done to their disadvantage.

In reply, still through a third person, Seward sent them the famous message, over the precise meaning of which great debate has raged: "Faith as to Sumter fully kept; wait and see." If this infatuated dreamer still believed he could dominate Lincoln, still hoped at the last moment to arrest the expedition to Charleston, he was doomed to bitterest disappointment.

On the 9th of April, the expedition to Fort Sumter sailed, but without, as we have seen, the assistance of the much needed warship, the Powhatan. As all the world knows, the expedition had been too long delayed and it accomplished nothing. Before it arrived, the surrender of Sumter had been demanded and refused —and war had begun. During the bombardment of Sumter, the relief expedition appeared beyond the bar, but its commander had no vessels of such a character as to enable him to carry aid to the fortress. Furthermore, he had not been informed that the Powhatan had been detached from his squadron, and he expected to meet her at the mouth of the harbor. There his ships lay idle until the fort was surrendered, waiting for the Powhatan—for whose detachment from the squadron Seward was responsible.

To return to the world of intrigue at Washington, however, it must not be supposed, as is so often done, that Fort Sumter was the one concern of the new government during its first six weeks. In fact, the subject occupied but a fraction of Lincoln's time. Scarcely second in importance was that matter so curiously bound up with the relief of the forts—the getting in hand of the strangely vain glorious Secretary of State. Mention has already been made of All-Fools' Day, 1861. Several marvelous things took place on that day. Strangest of all was the presentation of a paper by the Secretary of State to his chief, entitled "Thoughts for the President's Consideration". Whether it be regarded as a state paper or as a biographical detail in the career of Seward, it proves to be quite the most astounding thing in the whole episode. The "Thoughts" outlined a course of policy by which the buoyant Secretary intended to make good his prophecy of domestic peace within ninety days. Besides calmly patronizing Lincoln, assuring him that his lack of "a policy either domestic or foreign" was "not culpable and ... even unavoidable," the paper warned him that "policies ... both domestic and foreign" must immediately be adopted, and it proceeded to point out what they ought to be. Briefly stated, the one true policy which he advocated at home was to evacuate Sumter (though Pickens for some unexplained reason might be safely retained) and then, in order to bring the Southerners back into the Union, to pick quarrels with both Spain and France; to proceed as quickly as possible to war with both powers; and to have the ultimate satisfaction of beholding the reunion of the country through the general enthusiasm that was bound to come. Finally, the paper intimated that the Secretary of State was the man to carry this project through to success.

All this is not opera bouffe, but serious history. It must have taxed Lincoln's sense of humor and strained his sense of the fitness of things to treat such nonsense with the tactful forbearance which he showed and to relegate it to the pigeonhole without making Seward angry. Yet this he contrived to do; and he also managed, gently but firmly, to make it plain that the President intended to exercise his authority as the chief magistrate of the nation. His forbearance was further shown in passing over without rebuke Seward's part in the affair of Sumter, which might so easily have been made to appear treacherous, and in shouldering himself with all responsibility for the failure of the Charleston expedition. In the wave of excitement following the surrender, even so debonair a minister as Seward must have realized how fortunate it was for him that his chief did not tell all he knew. About this time Seward began to perceive that Lincoln had a will of his own, and that it was not safe to trifle further with the President. Seward thereupon ceased his interference.

It was in the dark days preceding the fall of Sumter that a crowd of office-seekers gathered at Washington, most of them men who had little interest in anything but the spoils. It is a distressing commentary on the American party system that, during the most critical month of the most critical period of American history, much of the President's time was consumed by these political vampires who would not be put off, even though a revolution was in progress and nations, perhaps, were dying and being born. "The scramble for office," wrote Stanton, "is terrible." Seward noted privately: "Solicitants for office besiege the President... My duties call me to the White House two or three times a day. The grounds, halls, stairways, closets, are filled with applicants who render ingress and egress difficult."

Secretary Welles has etched the Washington of that time in his coldly scornful way:

"A strange state of things existed at that time in Washington. The atmosphere was thick with treason. Party spirit and old party differences prevailed, however, amidst these accumulated dangers. Secession was considered by most persons as a political party question, not as rebellion. Democrats to a large extent sympathized with the Rebels more than with the Administration, which they opposed, not that they wished Secession to be successful and the Union divided, but they hoped that President Lincoln and the Republicans would, overwhelmed by obstacles and embarrassments, prove failures. The Republicans on the other hand, were scarcely less partisan and unreasonable. Patriotism was with them no test, no shield from party malevolence. They demanded the proscription and exclusion of such Democrats as opposed the Rebel movement and clung to the Union, with the same vehemence that they demanded the removal of the worst Rebels who advocated a dissolution of the Union. Neither party appeared to be apprehensive of, or to realize the gathering storm."

Seen against such a background, the political and diplomatic frivolity of the Secretary of State is not so inexplicable as it would otherwise be. This background, as well as the intrigue of the Secretary, helps us to understand Lincoln's great task inside his Cabinet. At first the Cabinet was a group of jealous politicians new to this sort of office, drawn from different parties, and totally lacking in a cordial sense of previous action together. None of them, probably, when they first assembled had any high opinion of their titular head. He was looked upon as a political makeshift. The best of them had to learn to appreciate the fact that this strange, ungainly man, sprung from plainest origin, without formal education, was a great genius. By degrees, however, the large minds in the Cabinet became his cordial admirers. While Lincoln was quietly, gradually exercising his strong will upon Seward, he was doing the same with the other members of his council. Presently they awoke—the majority of them at least—to the truth that he, for all his odd ways, was their master.

Meanwhile the gradual readjustment of all factions in the North was steadily going forward. The Republicans were falling into line behind the Government; and by degrees the distinction between Seward and Lincoln, in the popular mind, faded into a sort of composite picture called "the Administration." Lincoln had the reward of his long forbearance with his Secretary. For Seward it must be said that, however he had intrigued against his chief at Washington, he did not intrigue with the country. Admitting as he had, too, that he had met his master, he took the defeat as a good sportsman and threw all his vast party influence into the scale for Lincoln's fortunes. Thus, as April wore on, the Republican party settled down to the idea that it was to follow the Government at Washington upon any course that might develop.

The Democrats in the North were anti-Southern in larger proportion, probably, than at any other time during the struggle of the sections. We have seen that numbers of them had frankly declared for the Union. Politics had proved weaker than propinquity. There was a moment when it seemed—delusively, as events proved—that the North was united as one man to oppose the South.

There is surely not another day in our history that has witnessed so much nervous tension as Saturday, April 13, 1861, for on that morning the newspapers electrified the North with the news that Sumter had been fired on from Confederate batteries on the shore of Charleston Harbor. In the South the issue was awaited confidently, but many minds at least were in that state of awed suspense natural to a moment which the thoughtful see is the stroke of fate. In the North, the day passed for the most part in a quiet so breathless that even the most careless could have foretold the storm which broke on the following day. The account of this crisis which has been given by Lincoln's private secretary is interesting:

"That day there was little change in the business routine of the Executive office. Mr. Lincoln was never liable to sudden excitement or sudden activity... So while the Sumter telegrams were on every tongue... leading men and officials called to learn or impart the news. The Cabinet, as by common impulse, came together and deliberated. All talk, however, was brief, sententious, formal. Lincoln said but little beyond making inquiries about the current reports and criticizing the probability or accuracy of their details, and went on as usual receiving visitors, listening to suggestions, and signing routine papers throughout the day." Meanwhile the cannon were booming at Charleston. The people came out on the sea-front of the lovely old city and watched the duel of the cannon far down the harbor, and spoke joyously of the great event. They saw the shells of the shore batteries ignite portions of the fortress on the island. They watched the fire of the defenders—driven by the flames into a restricted area—slacken and cease. At last the flag of the Union fluttered down from above Fort Sumter.

When the news flashed over the North, early Sunday morning, April 14th, the tension broke. For many observers then and afterward, the only North discernible that fateful Sabbath was an enraged, defiant, impulsive nation, forgetful for the moment of all its differences, and uniting all its voices in one hoarse cry for vengeance. There seemed to be no other thought. Lincoln gave it formal utterance, that same day, by assembling his Cabinet and drawing up a proclamation which called for 75,000 volunteer troops.

An incident of this day which is as significant historically as any other was on the surface no more than a friendly talk between two men. Douglas called at the White House. For nearly two hours he and Lincoln conferred in private. Hitherto it had been a little uncertain what course Douglas was going to take. In the Senate, though condemning disunion, he had opposed war. Few matters can have troubled Lincoln more deeply than the question which way Douglas's immense influence would be thrown. The question was answered publicly in the newspapers of Monday, April 15th. Douglas announced that while he was still "unalterably opposed to the Administration on all its political issues, he was prepared to sustain the President in the exercise of all his constitutional functions to preserve the Union, and maintain the Government, and defend the federal capital."

There remained of Douglas's life but a few months. The time was filled with earnest speechmaking in support of the Government. He had started West directly following his conference with Lincoln. His speeches in Ohio, Indiana, Illinois, were perhaps the greatest single force in breaking up his own following, putting an end to the principle of doing nothing, and forcing every Democrat to come out and show his colors. In Shakespeare's phrase, it was—"Under which king, Bezonian? speak or die!" In Douglas's own phrase: "There can be no neutrals in this war; ONLY PATRIOTS—OR TRAITORS."

Side by side with Douglas's manifesto to the Democrats there appeared in the Monday papers Lincoln's call for volunteers. The militia of several Northern States at once responded.

On Wednesday, the 17th of April, the Sixth Massachusetts Regiment entrained for Washington. Two days later it was in Baltimore. There it was attacked by a mob; the soldiers fired; and a number of civilians were killed as well as several soldiers.

These shots at Baltimore aroused the Southern party in Maryland. Led by the Mayor of the city, they resolved to prevent the passage of other troops across their State to Washington. Railway tracks were torn up by order of the municipal authorities, and bridges were burnt. The telegraph was cut. As in a flash, after issuing his proclamation, Lincoln found himself isolated at Washington with no force but a handful of troops and the government clerks. And while Maryland rose against him on one side,

Virginia joined his enemies on the other. The day the Sixth Massachusetts left Boston, Virginia seceded. The Virginia militia were called to their colors. Preparations were at once set on foot for the seizure of the great federal arsenal at Harper's Ferry and the Navy Yard at Norfolk. The next day a handful of federal troops, fearful of being overpowered at Harper's Ferry, burned the arsenal and withdrew to Washington. For the same reason the buildings of the great Navy Yard were blown up or set on fire, and the ships at anchor were sunk. So desperate and unprepared were the Washington authorities that they took these extreme measures to keep arms and ammunition out of the hands of the Virginians. So hastily was the destruction carried out, that it was only partially successful and at both places large stores of ammunition were seized by the Virginia troops. While Washington was isolated, and Lincoln did not know what response the North had made to his proclamation, Robert E. Lee, having resigned his commission in the federal army, was placed in command of the Virginia troops.

The secretaries of Lincoln have preserved a picture of his desperate anxiety, waiting, day after day, for relief from the North which he hoped would speedily come by sea. Outwardly he maintained his self-control. "But once, on the afternoon of the 23d, the business of the day being over, the Executive office being deserted, after walking the floor alone in silent thought for nearly half an hour, he stopped and gazed long and wistfully out of the window down the Potomac in the direction of the expected ships; and, unconscious of other presence in the room, at length broke out with irrepressible anguish in the repeated exclamation, "Why don't they come! Why don't they come!"

During these days of isolation, when Washington, with the telegraph inoperative, was kept in an appalling uncertainty, the North rose. There was literally a rush to volunteer. "The heather is on fire," wrote George Ticknor, "I never before knew what a popular excitement can be." As fast as possible militia were hurried South. The crack New York regiment, the famous, dandified Seventh, started for the front amid probably the most tempestuous ovation which until that time was ever given to a military organization in America. Of the march of the regiment down Broadway, one of its members wrote, "Only one who passed as we did, through the tempest of cheers two miles long, can know the terrible enthusiasm of the occasion."

To reach Washington by rail was impossible. The Seventh went by boat to Annapolis. The same course was taken by a regiment of Massachusetts mechanics, the Eighth. Landing at Annapolis, the two regiments, dandies and laborers, fraternized at once in the common bond of loyalty to the Union. A branch railway led from Annapolis to the main line between Washington and Baltimore. The rails had been torn up. The Massachusetts mechanics set to work to relay them. The Governor of Maryland protested. He was disregarded. The two regiments toiled together a long day and through the night following, between Annapolis and the Washington junction, bringing on their baggage and cannon over relaid tracks. There, a train was found which the Seventh appropriated. At noon, on the 25th of April, that advance guard of the Northern hosts entered Washington, and Lincoln knew that he had armies behind him.

CHAPTER VII.
LINCOLN

The history of the North had virtually become, by April, 1861, the history of Lincoln himself, and during the remaining four years of the President's life it is difficult to separate his personality from the trend of national history. Any attempt to understand the achievements and the omissions of the Northern people without undertaking an intelligent estimate of their leader would be only to duplicate the story of "Hamlet" with Hamlet left out. According to the opinion of English military experts[12], "Against the great military genius of certain Southern leaders fate opposed the unbroken resolution and passionate devotion to the Union, which he worshiped, of the great Northern President. As long as he lived and ruled the people of the North, there could be no turning back."

Lincoln has been ranked with Socrates; but he has also been compared with Rabelais. He has been the target of abuse that knew no mercy; but he has been worshiped as a demigod. The ten big volumes of his official biography are a sustained, intemperate eulogy in which the hero does nothing that is not admirable; but as large a book could be built up out of contemporaneous Northern writings that would paint a picture of unmitigated blackness—and the most eloquent portions of it would be signed by Wendell Phillips.

The real Lincoln is, of course, neither the Lincoln of the official

---

[12] Wood and Edmonds. "The Civil War in the United States."

biography nor the Lincoln of Wendell Phillips. He was neither a saint nor a villain. What he actually was is not, however, so easily stated. Prodigious men are never easy to sum up; and Lincoln was a prodigious man. The more one studies him, the more individual he appears to be. By degrees one comes to understand how it was possible for contemporaries to hold contradictory views of him and for each to believe frantically that his views were proved by facts. For anyone who thinks he can hit off in a few neat generalities this complex, extraordinary personality, a single warning may suffice. Walt Whitman, who was perhaps the most original thinker and the most acute observer who ever saw Lincoln face to face has left us his impression; but he adds that there was something in Lincoln's face which defied description and which no picture had caught. After Whitman's conclusion that "One of the great portrait painters of two or three hundred years ago is needed," the mere historian should proceed with caution.

There is historic significance in his very appearance. His huge, loose-knit figure, six feet four inches high, lean, muscular, ungainly, the evidence of his great physical strength, was a fit symbol of those hard workers, the children of the soil, from whom he sprang. His face was rugged like his figure, the complexion swarthy, cheek bones high, and bushy black hair crowning a great forehead beneath which the eyes were deep-set, gray, and dreaming. A sort of shambling powerfulness formed the main suggestion of face and figure, softened strangely by the mysterious expression of the eyes, and by the singular delicacy of the skin. The motions of this awkward giant lacked grace; the top hat and black frock coat, sometimes rusty, which had served him on the western circuit continued to serve him when he was virtually the dictator of his country. It was in such dress that he visited the army, where he towered above his generals.

Even in a book of restricted scope, such as this, one must insist upon the distinction between the private and public Lincoln, for there is as yet no accepted conception of him. What comes nearest to an accepted conception is contained probably in the version of the late Charles Francis Adams. He tells us how his father, the elder Charles Francis Adams, ambassador to London, found Lincoln in 1861 an offensive personality, and he insists that Lincoln under strain passed through a transformation which made the Lincoln of 1864 a different man from the Lincoln of 1861. Perhaps; but without being frivolous, one is tempted to quote certain old-fashioned American papers that used to label their news items "important if true."

What then, was the public Lincoln? What explains his vast success? As a force in American history, what does he count for? Perhaps the most significant detail in an answer to these questions is the fact that he had never held conspicuous public office until at the age of fifty-two he became President. Psychologically his place is in that small group of great geniuses whose whole significant period lies in what we commonly think of as the decline of life. There are several such in history: Rome had Caesar; America had both Lincoln and Lee. By contrasting these instances with those of the other type, the egoistic geniuses such as Alexander or Napoleon, we become aware of some dim but profound dividing line separating the two groups. The theory that genius, at bottom, is pure energy seems to fit Napoleon; but does it fit these other minds who appear to meet life with a certain indifference, with a carelessness of their own fate, a willingness to leave much to chance? That irresistible passion for authority which Napoleon had is lacking in these others. Their basal inspiration seems to resemble the impulse of the artist to express, rather than the impulse of the man of action to possess. Had it not been for secession, Lee would probably have ended his days as an exemplary superintendent of West Point. And what of Lincoln? He dabbled in politics, early and without success; he left politics for the law, and to the law he gave during many years his chief devotion. But the fortuitous break-up of parties, with the revival of the slavery issue, touched some hidden spring; the able provincial lawyer felt again the political impulse; he became a famous maker of political phrases; and on this literary basis he became the leader of a party.

Too little attention has been paid to this progression of Lincoln through literature into politics. The ease with which he drifted from one to the other is also still to be evaluated. Did it show a certain slackness, a certain aimlessness, at the bottom of his nature? Had it, in a way, some sort of analogy—to compare homespun with things Olympian—to the vein of frivolity in the great Caesar? One is tempted to think so. Surely, here was one of those natures which need circumstance to compel them to greatness and which are not foredoomed, Napoleon-like, to seize greatness. Without encroaching upon the biographical task, one may borrow from biography this insistent echo: the anecdotes of Lincoln sound over and over the note of easy-going good nature; but there is to be found in many of the Lincoln anecdotes an overtone of melancholy which lingers after one's impression of his good nature. Quite naturally, in such a biographical atmosphere, we find ourselves thinking of him at first as a little too good-humored, a little too easy-going, a little prone to fall into reverie. We are not surprised when we find his favorite poem beginning "Oh, why should the spirit of mortal be proud."

This enigmatical man became President in his fifty-second year. We have already seen that his next period, the winter of 1860-61, has its biographical problems. The impression which he made on the country as President-elect was distinctly unfavorable. Good humor, or opportunism, or what you will, brought together in Lincoln's Cabinet at least three men more conspicuous in the ordinary sense than he was himself. We forget, today, how insignificant he must have seemed in a Cabinet that embraced Seward, Cameron, and Chase—all large national figures. What would not history give for a page of self-revelation showing us how he felt in the early days of that company! Was he troubled? Did he doubt his ability to hold his own? Was he fatalistic? Was his sad smile his refuge? Did he merely put things by, ignoring tomorrow until tomorrow should arrive?

However we may guess at the answers to such questions, one thing now becomes certain. His quality of good humor began to be his salvation. It is doubtful if any President except Washington had to manage so difficult a Cabinet. Washington had seen no solution to the problem but to let Jefferson go. Lincoln found his Cabinet often on the verge of a split, with two powerful factions struggling to control it and neither ever gaining full control. Though there were numerous withdrawals, no resigning secretary really split Lincoln's Cabinet. By what turns and twists and skillful maneuvers Lincoln prevented such a division and kept such inveterate enemies as Chase and Seward steadily at their jobs—Chase during three years, Seward to the end—will partly appear in the following pages; but the whole delicate achievement cannot be properly appreciated except in detailed biography.

All criticism of Lincoln turns eventually on one question: Was he an opportunist? Not only his enemies in his own time but many politicians of a later day were eager to prove that he was the latter—indeed, seeking to shelter their own opportunism behind the majesty of his example. A modern instance will perhaps make vivid this long standing debate upon Lincoln and his motives. Merely for historic illumination and without becoming invidious, we may recall the instance of President Wilson and the resignation of his Secretary of War in 1916 because Congress would not meet the issue of preparedness. The President accepted the resignation without forcing the issue, and Congress went on fiddling while Rome burned. Now, was the President an opportunist, merely waiting to see what course events would take, or was he a political strategist, astutely biding his time? Similar in character is this old debate upon Lincoln, which is perhaps best focussed in the removal of Secretary Blair which we shall have to note in connection with the election of 1864.

It is difficult for the most objective historian to deal with such questions without obtruding his personal views, but there is nothing merely individual in recording the fact that the steady drift of opinion has been away from the conception of Lincoln as an opportunist. What once caused him to be thus conceived appears now to have been a failure to comprehend intelligently the nature of his undertaking. More and more, the tendency nowadays is to conceive his career as one of those few instances in which the precise faculties needed to solve a particular problem were called into play at exactly the critical moment. Our confusions with regard to Lincoln have grown out of our failure to appreciate the singularity of the American people, and their ultra-singularity during the years in which he lived. It remains to be seen hereafter what strange elements of sensibility, of waywardness, of lack of imagination, of undisciplined ardor, of selfishness, of deceitfulness, of treachery, combined with heroic ideality, made up the character of that complex populace which it was Lincoln's task to control. But he did more than control it: he somehow compounded much of it into something like a unit. To measure Lincoln's achievement in this respect, two things must be remembered: on the one hand, his task was not as arduous as it might have been, because the most intellectual part of the North had definitely committed itself either irretrievably for, or irreconcilably against, his policy. Lincoln, therefore, did not have to trouble himself with this portion of the population. On the other hand, that part which he had to master included such emotional rhetoricians as Horace Greeley; such fierce zealots as Henry Winter Davis of Maryland, who made him trouble indeed, and Benjamin Wade, whom we have met already; such military egoists as McClellan and Pope; such crafty double-dealers as his own Secretary of the Treasury; such astute grafters as Cameron; such miserable creatures as certain powerful capitalists who sacrificed his army to their own lust for profits filched from army contracts.

The wonder of Lincoln's achievement is that he contrived at last to extend his hold over all these diverse elements; that he persuaded some, outwitted others, and overcame them all. The subtlety of this task would have ruined any statesman of the driving sort. Explain Lincoln by any theory you will, his personality was the keystone of the Northern arch; subtract it, and the arch falls. The popular element being as complex and powerful as it was, how could the presiding statesman have mastered the situation if he had not been of so peculiar a sort that he could influence all these diverse and powerful interests, slowly, by degrees, without heat, without the imperative note, almost in silence, with the universal, enfolding irresistibility of the gradual things in nature, of the sun and the rain. Such was the genius of Lincoln—all but passionless, yet so quiet that one cannot but believe in the great depth of his nature.

We are, even today, far from a definitive understanding of Lincoln's statecraft, but there is perhaps justification for venturing upon one prophecy. The farther from him we get and the more clearly we see him in perspective, the more we shall realize his creative influence upon his party. A Lincoln who is the moulder of events and the great creator of public opinion will emerge at last into clear view. In the Lincoln of his ultimate biographer there will be more of iron than of a less enduring metal in the figure of the Lincoln of present tradition. Though none of his gentleness will disappear, there will be more emphasis placed upon his firmness, and upon such episodes as that of December, 1860, when his single will turned the scale against compromise; upon his steadiness in the defeat of his party at the polls in 1862; or his overruling of the will of Congress in the summer of 1864 on the question of reconstruction; or his attitude in the autumn of that year when he believed that he was losing his second election. Behind all his gentleness, his slowness, behind his sadness, there will eventually appear an inflexible purpose, strong as steel, unwavering as fate.

The Civil War was in truth Lincoln's war. Those modern pacifists who claim him for their own are beside the mark. They will never get over their illusions about Lincoln until they see, as all the world is beginning to see, that his career has universal significance because of its bearing on the universal modern problem of democracy. It will not do ever to forget that he was a man of the people, always playing the hand of the people, in the limited social sense of that word, though playing it with none of the heat usually met with in the statesmen of successful democracy from Cleon to

Robespierre, from Andrew Jackson to Lloyd George. His gentleness does not remove Lincoln from that stern category. Throughout his life, besides his passion for the Union, besides his antipathy to slavery, there dwelt in his very heart love of and faith in the plain people. We shall never see him in true historic perspective until we conceive him as the instrument of a vast social idea—the determination to make a government based on the plain people successful in war.

He did not scruple to seize power when he thought the cause of the people demanded it, and his enemies were prompt to accuse him of holding to the doctrine that the end justified the means—a hasty conclusion which will have to be reconsidered; what concerns us more closely is the definite conviction that he felt no sacrifice too great if it advanced the happiness of the generality of mankind.

The final significance of Lincoln as a statesman of democracy is brought out most clearly in his foreign relations. Fate put it into the hands of England to determine whether his Government should stand or fall. Though it is doubtful how far the turning of the scale of English policy in Lincoln's favor was due to the influence of the rising power of English democracy, it is plain that Lincoln thought of himself as having one purpose with that movement which he regarded as an ally. Beyond all doubt among the most grateful messages he ever received were the New Year greetings of confidence and sympathy which were sent by English workingmen in 1863. A few sentences in his "Letter to the Workingmen of London" help us to look through his eyes and see his life and its struggles as they appeared to him in relation to world history:

> "As these sentiments [expressed by the English workmen] are manifestly the enduring support of the free institutions of England, so am I sure that they constitute the only reliable basis for free institutions throughout the world . . . The resources, advantages, and power of the American people are very great, and they have consequently succeeded to equally great responsibilities. It seems to have devolved upon them to test whether a government established on the principles of human freedom can be maintained against an effort to build one upon the exclusive foundation of human bondage. They will rejoice with me in the new evidence which your proceedings furnish that the magnanimity they are exhibiting is justly estimated by the true friends of freedom and humanity in foreign countries."

Written at the opening of that terrible year, 1863, these words are a forward link with those more celebrated words spoken toward its close at Gettysburg. Perhaps at no time during the war, except during the few days immediately following his own reelection a year later, did Lincoln come so near being free from care as then. Perhaps that explains why his fundamental literary power reasserted itself so remarkably, why this speech of his at the dedication of the National Cemetery at Gettysburg on the 19th of November, 1863, remains one of the most memorable orations ever delivered:

> "Fourscore and seven years ago our fathers brought forth upon this continent a new nation, conceived in liberty, and dedicated to the proposition that all men are created equal.
>
> "Now we are engaged in a great civil war, testing whether that nation, or any nation so conceived and so dedicated, can long endure. We are met on a great battlefield of that war. We have come to dedicate a portion of that field as a final resting-place for those who here gave their lives that that nation might live. It is altogether fitting and proper that we should do this.
>
> "But in a larger sense we cannot dedicate, we cannot consecrate, we cannot hallow this ground. The brave men, living and dead, who struggled here, have consecrated it far above our power to add or detract. The world will little note nor long remember what we say here, but it can never forget what they did here. It is for us, the living, rather, to be dedicated here to the unfinished work which they who fought here have thus far so nobly advanced. It is rather for us to be here dedicated to the great task remaining before us: that from these honored dead we take increased devotion to that cause for which they gave the last full measure of devotion; that we here highly resolve that these dead shall not have died in vain; that this nation, under God, shall have a new birth of freedom; and that government of the people, by the people, and for the people, shall not perish from the earth."

CHAPTER VIII.
THE RULE OF LINCOLN

The fundamental problem of the Lincoln Government was the raising of armies, the sudden conversion of a community which was essentially industrial into a disciplined military organization. The accomplishment of so gigantic a transformation taxed the abilities of two Secretaries of War. The first, Simon Cameron, owed his place in the Cabinet to the double fact of being one of the ablest of political bosses and of standing high among Lincoln's competitors for the Presidential nomination. Personally honest, he was also a political cynic to whom tradition ascribes the epigram defining an honest politician as one who "when he is bought, will stay bought." As Secretary of War he showed no particular ability.

In 1861, when the tide of enthusiasm was in flood, and volunteers in hosts were responding to acts of Congress for the raising and maintenance of a volunteer army, Cameron reported in December that the Government had on foot 660,971 men and could have had a million except that Congress had limited the number of volunteers to be received. When this report was prepared, Lincoln was, so to speak, in the trough of two seas. The devotion which had been offered to him in April, 1861, when the North seemed to rise as one man, had undergone a reaction. Eight months without a single striking military success, together with the startling defeat at Bull Run, had had their inevitable effect. Democracies are mercurial; variability seems to be part of the price of freedom. With childlike faith in their cause, the Northern people, in midsummer, were crying, "On to Richmond!" In the autumn, stung by defeat, they were ready to cry, "Down with Lincoln."

In a subsequent report, the War Department confessed that at the beginning of hostilities, "nearly all our arms and ammunition" came from foreign countries. One great reason why no military successes relieve the gloom of 1861 was that, from a soldier's point of view, there were no armies. Soldiers, it is true, there were in myriads; but arms, ammunition, and above all, organization were lacking. The supplies in the government arsenals had been provided for an army of but a few thousand. Strive as they would, all the factories in the country could not come anywhere near making arms for half a million men; nor did the facilities of those days make it possible for munition plants to spring up overnight. Had it not been that the Confederacy was equally hard pushed, even harder pushed, to find arms and ammunition, the war would have ended inside Seward's ninety days, through sheer lack of powder.

Even with the respite given by the unpreparedness of the South, and while Lincoln hurriedly collected arms and ammunition from abroad, the startled nation, thus suddenly forced into a realization of what war meant, lost its head. From its previous reckless trust in sheer enthusiasm, it reacted to a distrust of almost everything. Why were the soldiers not armed? Why did not millions of rounds of cartridges fall like manna out of the sky? Why did not the crowds of volunteers become armies at a word of command? One of the darkest pages in American history records the way in which the crowd, undisciplined to endure strain, turned upon Lincoln in its desire to find in the conduct of their leader a pretext for venting upon him the fierceness of their anxiety. Such a pretext they found in his treatment of Fremont.

The singular episode of Fremont's arrogance in 1861 is part of the story of the border States whose friendship was eagerly sought by both sides—Maryland, Kentucky, Missouri, and those mountainous counties which in time were to become West Virginia. To retain Maryland and thus to keep open the connection between the Capital and the North was one of Lincoln's deepest anxieties. By degrees the hold of the Government in Maryland was made secure, and the State never seceded. Kentucky, too, held to the Union, though, during many anxious months in 1861, Lincoln did not know whether this State was to be for him or against him. The Virginia mountains, from the first, seemed a more hopeful field, for the mountaineers had opposed the Virginia secession and, as soon as it was accomplished, had begun holding meetings of protest. In the meantime George B. McClellan, with the rank of general bestowed upon him by the Federal Government, had been appointed to command the militia of Ohio. He was sent to assist the insurgent mountaineers, and with him went the Ohio militia. From this situation and from the small engagements with Confederate forces in which McClellan was successful, there resulted the separate State of West Virginia and the extravagant popular notion that McClellan was a great general. His successes were contrasted in the ordinary mind with the crushing defeat at Bull Run, which happened at about the same time.

The most serious of all these struggles in the border States, however, was that which took place in Missouri, where, owing to the strength of both factions and their promptness in organizing, real war began immediately. A Union army led by General Nathaniel Lyon attacked the Confederates with great spirit at Wilson's Creek but was beaten back in a fierce and bloody battle in which their leader was killed.

Even before these events Fremont had been appointed to chief command in Missouri, and here he at once began a strange course of dawdling and posing. His military career must be left to the military historians—who have not ranked him among the great generals. Civil history accuses him, if not of using his new position to make illegitimate profits, at least of showing reckless favoritism toward those who did. It is hardly unfair to say that Lincoln, in bearing with Fremont as long as he did, showed a touch of amiable weakness; and yet, it must be acknowledged that the President knew that the country was in a dangerous mood, that Fremont was immensely popular, and that any change might be misunderstood. Though Lincoln hated to appear anything but a friend to a fallen political rival, he was at last forced to act. Frauds in government contracts at St. Louis were a public scandal, and the reputation of the government had to be saved by the removal of Fremont in November, 1861. As an immediate consequence of this action the overstrained nerves of great numbers of people snapped. Fremont's personal followers, as well as the abolitionists whom he had actively supported while in command in Missouri, and all that vast crowd of excitable people who are unable to stand silent under strain, clamored against Lincoln in the wildest and most absurd vein. He was accused of being a "dictator"; he was called an "imbecile"; he ought to be impeached, and a new party, with Fremont as its leader, should be formed to prosecute the war. But through all this clamor Lincoln kept his peace and let the heathen rage.

Toward the end of the year, popular rage turned suddenly on Cameron, who, as Secretary of War, had taken an active but proper part in the investigation of Fremont's conduct. It was one of those tremulous moments when people are desperately eager to have something done and are ready to believe anything. Though McClellan, now in chief command of the Union forces, had an immense army which was fast getting properly equipped, month faded into month without his advancing against the enemy. Again the popular cry was raised, "On to Richmond!" It was at this moment of military inactivity and popular restlessness that charges of peculation were brought forward against Cameron.

These charges both were and were not well founded. Himself a rich man, it is not likely that Cameron profited personally by government contracts, even though the acrimonious Thad Stevens said of his appointment as Secretary that it would add "another million to his fortune." There seems little doubt, however, that Cameron showered lucrative contracts upon his political retainers. And no boss has ever held the State of Pennsylvania in a firmer grip. His tenure of the Secretaryship of War was one means to that end.

The restless alarm of the country at large expressed itself in such extravagant words as these which Senator Grimes wrote to Senator Fessenden: "We are going to destruction as fast as imbecility, corruption, and the wheels of time can carry us." So dissatisfied, indeed, was Congress with the conduct of the war that it appointed a committee of investigation. During December, 1861, and January, 1862, the committee was summoning generals before it, questioning them, listening to all manner of views, accomplishing nothing, but rendering more and more feverish an atmosphere already surcharged with anxiety. On the floors of Congress debate raged as to who was responsible for the military inaction—for the country's "unpreparedness," we should say today —and as to whether Cameron was honest. Eventually the House in a vote of censure condemned the Secretary of War.

Long before this happened, however, Lincoln had interfered and very characteristically removed the cause of trouble, while taking upon himself the responsibility for the situation, by nominating Cameron minister to Russia, and by praising him for his "ability, patriotism, and fidelity to the public trust." Though the President had not sufficient hold upon the

House to prevent the vote of censure, his influence was strong in the Senate, and the new appointment of Cameron was promptly confirmed.

There was in Washington at this time that grim man who had served briefly as Attorney-General in the Cabinet of Buchanan—Edwin M. Stanton. He despised the President and expressed his opinion in such words as "the painful imbecility of Lincoln." The two had one personal recollection in common: long before, in a single case, at Cincinnati, the awkward Lincoln had been called in as associate counsel to serve the convenience of Stanton, who was already a lawyer of national repute. To his less-known associate Stanton showed a brutal rudeness that was characteristic. It would have been hard in 1861 to find another man more difficult to get on with. Headstrong, irascible, rude, he had a sharp tongue which he delighted in using; but he was known to be inflexibly honest, and was supposed to have great executive ability. He was also a friend of McClellan, and if anybody could rouse that tortoise-like general, Stanton might be supposed to be the man. He had been a valiant Democrat, and Democratic support was needed by the government. Lincoln astonished him with his appointment as Secretary of War in January, 1862. Stanton justified the President's choice, and under his strong if ruthless hand the War Department became sternly efficient. The whole story of Stanton's relations to his chief is packed, like the Arabian genius in the fisherman's vase, into one remark of Lincoln's. "Did Stanton tell you I was a fool?" said Lincoln on one occasion, in the odd, smiling way he had. "Then I expect I must be one, for he is almost always right, and generally says what he means."

In spite of his efficiency and personal force, Stanton was unable to move his friend McClellan, with whom he soon quarreled. Each now sought in his own way to control the President, though neither understood Lincoln's character. From McClellan, Lincoln endured much condescension of a kind perilously near impertinence. To Stanton, Lincoln's patience seemed a mystery; to McClellan—a vain man, full of himself—the President who would merely smile at this bullyragging on the part of one of his subordinates seemed indeed a spiritless creature. Meanwhile Lincoln, apparently devoid of sensibility, was seeking during the anxious months of 1862, in one case, merely how to keep his petulant Secretary in harness; in the other, how to quicken his tortoise of a general.

Stanton made at least one great blunder. Though he had been three months in office, and McClellan was still inactive, there were already several successes to the credit of the Union arms. The Monitor and Virginia (Merrimac) had fought their famous duel, and Grant had taken Fort Donelson. The latter success broke through the long gloom of the North and caused, as Holmes wrote, "a delirium of excitement." Stanton rashly concluded that he now had the game in his hands, and that a sufficient number of men had volunteered. This civilian Secretary of War, who had still much to learn of military matters, issued an order putting a stop to recruiting. Shortly afterwards great disaster befell the Union arms. McClellan, before Richmond, was checked in May. Early in July, his peninsula campaign ended disastrously in the terrible "Seven Days' Battle."

Anticipating McClellan's failure, Lincoln had already determined to call for more troops. On July 1st, he called upon the Governors of the States to provide him with 300,000 men to serve three years. But the volunteering enthusiasm—explain it as you will—had suffered a check. The psychological moment had passed. So slow was the response to the call of July 1st, that another appeal was made early in August, this time for 300,000 men to serve only nine months. But this also failed to rouse the country. A reinforcement of only 87,000 men was raised in response to this emergency call. The able lawyer in the War Department had still much to learn about men and nations.

After this check, terrible incidents of war came thick and fast—the defeat at Second Manassas, in late August; the horrible drawn battle of Antietam-Sharpsburg, in September; Fredericksburg, that carnival of slaughter, in December; the dearly bought victory of Murfreesboro, which opened 1863. There were other disastrous events at least as serious. Foreign affairs[13] were at their darkest. Within the political coalition supporting Lincoln, contention was the order of the day. There was general distrust of the President. Most alarming of all, that ebb of the wave of enthusiasm which began in midsummer, 1861, reached in the autumn of 1862 perhaps its lowest point. The measure of the reaction against Lincoln was given in the Congressional election, in which, though the Government still retained a working majority, the Democrats gained thirty-three seats.

If there could be such a thing as a true psychological history of the war,

---

[13] See Chapter IX.

one of its most interesting pages would determine just how far Stanton was responsible, through his strange blunder over recruiting, for the check to enthusiasm among the Northern people. With this speculation there is connected a still unsolved problem in statistics. To what extent did the anti-Lincoln vote, in 1862, stand for sympathy with the South, and how far was it the hopeless surrender of Unionists who felt that their cause was lost? Though certainty on this point is apparently impossible, there can be no doubt that at the opening of 1863, the Government felt it must apply pressure to the flagging spirits of its supporters. In order to reenforce the armies and to push the war through, there was plainly but one course to be followed—conscription.

The government leaders in Congress brought in a Conscription Act early in the year. The hot debates upon this issue dragged through a month's time, and now make instructive reading for the present generation that has watched the Great War[14]. The Act of 1863 was not the work of soldiers, but was literally "made in Congress." Stanton grimly made the best of it, though he unwaveringly condemned some of its most conspicuous provisions. His business was to retrieve his blunder of the previous year, and he was successful. Imperfect as it was, the Conscription Act, with later supplementary legislation, enabled him to replace the wastage of the Union armies and steadily to augment them. At the close of the war, the Union had on foot a million men with an enrolled reserve of two millions and a half, subject to call.

The Act provided for a complete military census, for which purpose the country was divided into enrollment districts. Every able-bodied male citizen, or intending citizen, between the ages of twenty and forty-five, unless exempted for certain specified reasons, was to be enrolled as a member of the national forces; these forces were to be called to the colors—"drafted," the term was—as the Government found need of them; each successive draft was to be apportioned among the districts in the ratio of the military population, and the number required was to be drawn

---

[14] The battle over conscription in England was anticipated in America sixty-four years ago. Bagot says that the average British point of view may be expressed thus: "What I am sayin' is this here as I was a sayin' yesterday." The Anglo-Saxon mind is much the same the world over. In America, today, the enemies of effective military organization would do well to search the arguments of their skillful predecessors in 1888, who fought to the last ditch for a military system that would make inescapable "peace at any price." For the modern believers in conscription, one of their best bits of political thunder is still the defense of it by Lincoln.

by lot; if the district raised its quota voluntarily, no draft would be made; any drafted man could offer a substitute or could purchase his discharge for three hundred dollars. The latter provision especially was condemned by Stanton. It was seized upon by demagogues as a device for giving rich men an advantage over poor men.

American politics during the war form a wildly confused story, so intricate that it cannot be made clear in a brief statement. But this central fact may be insisted upon: in the North, there were two political groups that were the poles around which various other groups revolved and combined, only to fly asunder and recombine, with all the maddening inconstancy of a kaleidoscope. The two irreconcilable elements were the "war party" made up of determined men resolved to see things through, and the "copperheads"[15] who for one reason or another united in a faithful struggle for peace at any price. Around the copperheads gathered the various and singular groups who helped to make up the ever fluctuating "peace party." It is an error to assume that this peace party was animated throughout by fondness for the Confederacy. Though many of its members were so actuated, the core of the party seems to have been that strange type of man who sustained political evasion in the old days, who thought that sweet words can stop bullets, whose programme in 1863 called for a cessation of hostilities and a general convention of all the States, and who promised as the speedy result of a debauch of talk a carnival of bright eyes glistening with the tears of revived affection. With these strange people in 1863 there combined a number of different types: the still stranger, still less creditable visionary, of whom much hereafter; the avowed friends of the principle of state rights; all those who distrusted the Government because of its anti-slavery sympathies; Quakers and others with moral scruples against war; and finally, sincere legalists to whom the Conscription Act appeared unconstitutional. In the spring of 1863 the issue of conscription drew the line fairly sharply between the two political coalitions, though each continued to fluctuate, more or less, to the end of the war.

The peace party of 1863 has been denounced hastily rather than carefully studied. Its precise machinations are not fully known, but the ugly

---

[15] The term arose, it has been said, from the use of the copper cent with its head of Liberty as a peace button. But a more plausible explanation associates the peace advocates with the deadly copperhead snake.

fact stands forth that a portion of the foreign population of the North was roused in 1863 to rebellion. The occasion was the beginning of the first draft under the new law, in July, 1863, and the scene of the rebellion was the City of New York. The opponents of conscription had already made inflammatory attacks on the Government. Conspicuous among them was Horatio Seymour, who had been elected Governor of New York in that wave of reaction in the autumn of 1862. Several New York papers joined the crusade. In Congress, the Government had already been threatened with civil war if the act was enforced. Nevertheless, the public drawing by lot began on the days announced. In New York the first drawing took place on Saturday, July 12th, and the lists were published in the Sunday papers. As might be expected, many of the men drawn were of foreign birth, and all day Sunday, the foreign quarter of New York was a cauldron boiling.

On Monday, the resumption of the drawing was the signal for revolt. A mob invaded one of the conscription offices, drove off the men in charge, and set fire to the building. In a short while, the streets were filled with dense crowds of foreignborn workmen shouting, "Down with the rich men," and singing, "We'll hang Horace Greeley on a sour apple tree." Houses of prominent citizens were attacked and set on fire, and several drafting offices were burned. Many negroes who were seized were either clubbed to death or hanged to lamp posts. Even an orphan asylum for colored children was burned. The office of the "Tribune" was raided, gutted, and set on fire. Finally a dispatch to Stanton, early in the night, reported that the mob had taken possession of the city.

The events of the next day were no less shocking. The city was almost stripped of soldiers, as all available reserves had already been hurried south when Lee was advancing toward Gettysburg. But such militia as could be mustered, with a small force of federal troops, fought the mob in the streets. Barricades were carried by storm; blood was freely shed. It was not, however, until the fourth day that the rebellion was finally quelled, chiefly by New York regiments, hurried north by Stanton—among them the famous Seventh—which swept the streets with cannon.

The aftermath of the New York riots was a correspondence between Lincoln and Seymour. The latter had demanded a suspension of the draft until the courts could decide on the constitutionality of the Conscription Act. Lincoln refused. With ten thousand troops now assembled in New York, the draft was resumed, and there was no further trouble.

The resistance to the Government in New York was but the most terrible episode in a protracted contention which involves, as Americans are beginning to see, one of the most fundamental and permanent questions of Lincoln's rule: how can the exercise of necessary war powers by the President be reconciled with the guarantees of liberty in the Constitution? It is unfortunate that Lincoln did not draw up a fully rounded statement of his own theory regarding this problem, instead of leaving it to be inferred from detached observations and from his actions. Apparently, he felt there was nothing to do but to follow the Roman precedent and, in a case of emergency, frankly permit the use of extraordinary power. We may attribute to him that point of view expressed by a distinguished Democrat of our own day: "Democracy has to learn how to use the dictator as a necessary war tool."[16] Whether Lincoln set a good model for democracy in this perilous business is still to be determined. His actions have been freely labeled usurpation. The first notorious instance occurred in 1861, during the troubles in Maryland, when he authorized military arrests of suspected persons. For the release of one of these, a certain Merryman, Chief Justice Taney issued a writ of habeas corpus[17]. Lincoln authorized his military representatives to disregard the writ. In 1862 he issued a proclamation suspending the privileges of the writ of habeas corpus in cases of persons charged with "discouraging volunteer enlistments, resisting military drafts, or guilty of any disloyal practice . . . " Such persons were to be tried by military commissions.

There can be little doubt that this proclamation caused something like a panic in many minds, filled them with the dread of military despotism, and contributed to the reaction against Lincoln in the autumn of 1862. Under this proclamation many arrests were made and many victims were

---

[16] President Edwin A. Alderman, of the University of Virginia.

[17] The Constitution permits the suspension of the privileges of the writ of habeas corpus "when in cases of rebellion or invasion the public safety may require it," but fails to provide a method of suspension. Taney held that the power to suspend lay with Congress. Five years afterward, when Chase was Chief Justice, the Supreme Court, in ex parte Milligan, took the same view and further declared that even Congress could not deprive a citizen of his right to trial by jury so long as the local civil courts are in operation. The Confederate experience differed from the Federal inasmuch as Congress kept control of the power to suspend the writ. But both governments made use of such suspension to set up martial law in districts where the local courts were open but where, from one cause or another, the Administration had not confidence in their effectiveness. Under ex parte Milligan, both Presidents and both Congresses were guilty of usurpation. The mere layman waits for the next great hour of trial to learn whether this interpretation will stand. In the Milligan case the Chief Justice and three others dissented.

sent to prison. So violent was the opposition that on March 3, 1863, Congress passed an act which attempted to bring the military and civil courts into cooperation, though it did not take away from the President all the dictatorial power which he had assumed. The act seems, however, to have had little general effect, and it was disregarded in the most celebrated of the cases of military arrest, that of Clement L. Vallandigham.

A representative from Ohio and one of the most vituperative anti-Lincoln men in Congress, Vallandigham in a sensational speech applied to the existing situation Chatham's words, "My lords, you cannot conquer America." He professed to see before him in the future nothing "but universal political and social revolution, anarchy, and bloodshed, compared with which the Reign of Terror in France was a merciful visitation." To escape such a future, he demanded an armistice, to be followed by a friendly peace established through foreign mediation.

Returning to Ohio after the adjournment of Congress, Vallandigham spoke to a mass-meeting in a way that was construed as rank treason by General Burnside who was in command at Cincinnati. Vallandigham was arrested, tried by court martial, and condemned to imprisonment. There was an immediate hue and cry, in consequence of which Burnside, who reported the affair, felt called upon also to offer to resign. Lincoln's reply was characteristic: "When I shall wish to supersede you I shall let you know. All the Cabinet regretted the necessity for arresting, for instance, Vallandigham, some perhaps doubting there was a real necessity for it; but being done, all were for seeing you through with it." Lincoln, however, commuted the sentence to banishment and had Vallandigham sent through the lines into the Confederacy.

It seems quite plain that the condemnation of Lincoln on this issue of usurpation was not confined to the friends of the Confederacy, nor has it been confined to his enemies in later days. One of Lincoln's most ardent admirers, the historian Rhodes, condemns his course unqualifiedly. "There can be no question," he writes, "that from the legal point of view the President should have rescinded the sentence and released Vallandigham." Lincoln, he adds, "stands responsible for the casting into prison of citizens of the United States on orders as arbitrary as the lettres-de-cachet of Louis XIV." Since Mr. Rhodes, uncompromising Unionist, can write as he does upon this issue, it is plain that the opposition party cannot be dismissed as through and through disunionist.

The trial of Vallandigham made him a martyr and brought him the

Democratic nomination for Governor of Ohio[18]. His followers sought to make the issue of the campaign the acceptance or rejection of military despotism. In defense of his course Lincoln wrote two public letters in which he gave evidence of the skill which he had acquired as a lawyer before a jury by the way in which he played upon the emotions of his readers.

"Long experience [he wrote] has shown that armies cannot be maintained unless desertion shall be punished by the severe penalty of death. The case requires, and the law and the Constitution sanction, this punishment. Must I shoot a simple-minded soldier boy who deserts, while I must not touch a hair of a wily agitator who induces him to desert? This is none the less injurious when effected by getting a father, or brother, or friend into a public meeting, and there working upon his feelings till he is persuaded to write the soldier boy that he is fighting in a bad cause for a wicked administration and a contemptible government, too weak to arrest and punish him if he shall desert. I think that in such a case to silence the agitator and save the boy is not only constitutional, but, withal, a great mercy."

His real argument may be summed up in these words of his:

"You ask, in substance, whether I really claim that I may override all the guaranteed rights of individuals, on the plea of conserving the public safety—when I may choose to say the public safety requires it. This question, divested of the phraseology calculated to represent me as struggling for an arbitrary prerogative, is either simply a question who shall decide, or an affirmation that nobody shall decide, what the public safety does require in cases of rebellion or invasion.

"The Constitution contemplates the question as likely to occur for decision, but it does not expressly declare who is to decide it. By necessary implication, when rebellion or invasion comes, the decision is to be made, from time to time; and I think the man, whom for the time, the people have under the Constitution, made the commander-in-chief of their army and navy, is the man who holds the power and bears the responsibility of

---

[18] Edward Everett Hale's famous story "The Man Without a Country", though it got into print too late to affect the election, was aimed at Vallandigham. That quaint allegory on the lack of patriotism became a temporary classic.

making it. If he uses the power justly, the same people will probably justify him; if he abuses it, he is in their hands to be dealt with by all the modes they have reserved to themselves in the Constitution."

Lincoln virtually appealed to the Northern people to secure efficiency by setting him momentarily above all civil authority. He asked them in substance, to interpret their Constitution by a show of hands. No thoughtful person can doubt the risks of such a method; yet in Ohio, in 1863, the great majority—perhaps everyone who believed in the war—accepted Lincoln's position. Between their traditional system of legal juries and the new system of military tribunals the Ohio voters made their choice without hesitation. They rejected Vallandigham and sustained the Lincoln candidate by a majority of over a hundred thousand. That same year in New York the anti-Lincoln candidate for Secretary of State was defeated by twenty-nine thousand votes.

Though these elections in 1863 can hardly be called the turning-point in the history of the Lincoln Government, yet it was clear that the tide of popularity which had ebbed so far away from Lincoln in the autumn of 1862 was again in the flood. Another phase of his stormy course may be thought of as having ended. And in accounting for this turn of the tide it must not be forgotten that between the nomination and the defeat of a Vallandigham the bloody rebellion in New York had taken place, Gettysburg had been fought, and Grant had captured Vicksburg. The autumn of 1863 formed a breathing space for the war party of the North.

CHAPTER IX.
THE CRUCIAL MATTER

It is the custom of historians to measure the relative strength of North and South chiefly in terms of population. The North numbered 23,000,000 inhabitants; the South, about 9,000,000, of which the slave population amounted to 3,500,000. But these obvious statistics only partially indicate the real situation. Not what one has, but what one is capable of using is, of course, the true measure of strength. If, in 1861, either side could have struck swiftly and with all its force, the story of the war would have been different. The question of relative strength was in reality a question of munitions. Both powers were glaringly unprepared. Both had instant need of great supplies of arms and ammunition, and both turned to European manufacturers for aid. Those Americans who, in a later war, wished to make illegal the neutral trade in munitions forgot that the international right of a belligerent to buy arms from a neutral had prevented their own destruction in 1861. In the supreme American crisis, agents of both North and South hurried to Europe in quest of munitions. On the Northern side the work was done chiefly by the three ministers, Charles Francis Adams, at London; William L. Dayton, at Paris; and Henry S. Sanford, at Brussels; by an able special agent, Colonel George L. Schuyler; and by the famous banking-house of Baring Brothers, which one might almost have called the European department of the United States Treasury.

The eager solicitude of the War Department over the competition of the two groups of agents in Europe informs a number of dispatches that are, today, precious admonitions to the heedless descendants of that dreadful time. As late as October, 1861, the Acting Secretary of War wrote to Schuyler, one of whose shipments had been delayed: "The Department earnestly hopes to receive ... the 12,000 Enfield rifles and the remainder of the 27,000, which you state you have purchased, by the earliest steamer following. Could you appreciate the circumstances by which we are surrounded, you would readily understand the urgent necessity there is for the immediate delivery of all the arms you are authorized to purchase. The Department expects to hear that you have been able to conclude the negotiations for the 48,000 rifles from the French government arsenals." That the Confederate Government acted even more promptly than the Union Government appears from a letter of Sanford to Seward in May: "I have vainly expected orders," he complains, "for the purchase of arms for the Government, and am tempted to order from Belgium all they can send over immediately . . . Meanwhile the workshops are filling with orders from the South . . . It distresses me to think that while we are in want of them, Southern money is taking them away to be used against us."

At London, Adams took it upon himself to contract for arms in advance of instructions. He wrote to Seward: "Aware of the degree to which I exceed my authority in taking such a step, nothing but a conviction of the need in which the country stands of such assistance and the joint opinion of all the diplomatic agents of the United States ... in Paris, has induced me to overcome my scruples." How real was the necessity of which this able diplomat was so early conscious, is demonstrated at every turn in the papers of the War Department. Witness this brief dispatch from Harrisburg: "All ready to leave but no arms. Governor not willing to let us leave State without them, as act of Assembly forbids. Can arms be sent here?" When this appeal was made, in December, 1861, arms were pouring into the country from Europe, and the crisis had passed. But if this appeal had been made earlier in the year, the inevitable answer may be guessed from a dispatch which the Ordnance Office sent, as late as September, to the authorities of West Virginia, refusing to supply them with arms because the supplies were exhausted, and adding, "Every possible exertion is being made to obtain additional supplies by contract, by manufacture, and by purchase, and as soon as they can be procured by any means, in any way, they will be supplied."

Curiously enough, not only the Confederacy but various States of the

North were more expeditious in this all-important matter than Cameron and the War Department. Schuyler's first dispatch from London gives this singular information: "All private establishments in Birmingham and London are now working for the States of Ohio, Connecticut, and Massachusetts, except the London Armory, whose manufacture is supposed to go to the Rebels, but of this last fact I am not positively informed. I am making arrangements to secure these establishments for our Government, if desirable after the present State contracts expire. On the Continent, Messrs, Dayton and Sanford ... have been making contracts and agreements of various kinds, of which you are by this time informed." Soon afterward, from Paris, he made a long report detailing the difficulties of his task, the limitations of the existing munitions plants in Europe, and promising among other things those "48,000 rifles from the French government arsenals" for which, in the letter already quoted, the War Department yearned. It was an enormous labor; and, strive as he would, Schuyler found American mail continuing to bring him such letters as this from the Assistant Secretary of War in October: "I notice with much regret that [in the latest consignment] there were no guns sent, as it was confidently expected that 20,000 would arrive by the [steamship] Fulton, and accordingly arrangements had been made to distribute them through the different States. Prompt and early shipments of guns are desirable. We hope to hear by next steamer that you have shipped from 80,000 to 100,000 stand."

The last word on the problem of munitions, which was so significant a factor in the larger problem, is the report of the United States Ordnance Office for the first year of the war. It shows that between April, 1861, and June, 1862, the Government purchased from American manufacturers somewhat over 30,000 rifles, and that from European makers it purchased 726,000.

From these illustrations it is therefore obvious that the true measure of the immediate strength of the American contestants in 1861 was the extent of their ability to supply themselves from Europe; and this, stated more concretely, became the question as to which was the better able to keep its ports open and receive the absolutely essential European aid. Lincoln showed his clear realization of the situation when he issued, immediately after the first call for volunteers, a proclamation blockading the Southern coasts. Whether the Northern people at the time appreciated the significance of this order is a question. Amid the wild and vain clamor of the multitude in 1861, with its conventional and old-fashioned notion of war as a thing of trumpets and glittering armies, the North seems wholly to have ignored its fleet; and yet in the beginning this resource was its only strength.

The fleet was small, to be sure, but its task was at first also small. There were few Southern ports which were doing a regular business with Europe, and to close these was not difficult. As other ports opened and the task of blockade grew, the Northern navy also increased. Within a few months, to the few observers who did not lose their heads, it was plain that the North had won the first great contest of the war. It had so hampered Southern trade that Lincoln's advantage in arming the North from Europe was ten to one. At the very time when detractors of Lincoln were hysterical over the removal of Fremont, when Grimes wrote to Fessenden that the country was going to the dogs as fast as imbecility could carry it, this great achievement had quietly taken place. An expedition sailing in August from Fortress Monroe seized the forts which commanded Hatteras Inlet off the coast of North Carolina. In November, Commander Dupont, U. S. N., seized Port Royal, one of the best harbors on the coast of South Carolina, and established there a naval base. Thenceforth, while the open Northern ports received European munitions without hindrance, it was a risky business getting munitions into the ports of the South. Only the boldest traders would attempt to "run the blockade," to evade the Federal patrol ships by night and run into a Southern port.

However, for one moment in the autumn of 1861, it seemed as if all the masterful work of the Northern navy would be undone by the Northern people themselves in backing up the rashness of Captain Charles Wilkes, of the war-ship San Jacinto. On the high seas he overhauled the British mail steamer, Trent. Aboard her were two Confederate diplomatic agents, James M. Mason and John Slidell, who had run the blockade from Charleston to Havana and were now on their way to England. Wilkes took off the two Confederates as prisoners of war. The crowd in the North went wild. "We do not believe," said the New York Times, "that the American heart ever thrilled with more sincere delight."

The intemperate joy of the crowd over the rashness of Wilkes was due in part to a feeling of bitterness against the British Government. In May, 1861, the Queen had issued a proclamation of neutrality, whose justification in international law was hotly debated at the time and was generally denied by Northerners. England was the great cotton market of the world. To the excited Northern mind, in 1861, there could be but one explanation of England's action: a partisan desire to serve the South, to break up the blockade, and to secure cotton. Whether such was the real purpose of the ministry then in power is now doubted; but at that time it was the beginning of a sharp contention between the two Governments. The Trent affair naturally increased the tension. So keen was the indignation of all classes of Englishmen that it seemed, for a moment, as if the next step would be war.

In America, the prompt demand for the release of Mason and Slidell was met, at first, in a spirit equally bellicose. Fortunately there were cool and clear heads that at once condemned Wilkes's action as a gross breach of international law. Prominent among these was Sumner. The American Government, however, admitted the justice of the British demand and the envoys were released.

Relations with the United States now became a burning issue in English politics. There were three distinct groups in Parliament. The representatives of the aristocracy, whether Liberals or Conservatives, in the main sympathized with the South. So did most of the large manufacturers whose business interests were affected by cotton. Great bitterness grew up among the Northerners against both these groups, partly because in the past many of their members had condemned slavery and had said scornful things about America for tolerating it. To these Northerners the Englishmen replied that Lincoln himself had declared the war was not over slavery; that it was an ordinary civil war not involving moral issues. Nevertheless, the third Parliamentary group insisted that the American war, no matter what the motives of the participants, would, in the event of a Northern victory, bring about the abolition of slavery, whereas, if the South won, the result would be the perpetuation of slavery. This third group, therefore, threw all its weight on the side of the North. In this group Lincoln recognized his allies, and their cause he identified with his own in his letter to English workmen which was quoted in the previous chapter. Their leaders in Parliament were Richard Cobden, W. E. Forster, and John Bright. All these groups were represented in the Liberal party, which, for the moment, was in power.

In the Cabinet itself there was a "Northern" and a "Southern" faction. Then, too, there were some who sympathized with the North but who felt that its cause was hopeless—so little did they understand the relative strength of the two sections—and who felt that the war was a terrible proof of the uselessness of mere suffering. Gladstone, in later days, wished to be thought of as having been one of these, though at the time, a famous utterance of his was construed in the North as a declaration of hostility. To a great audience at Newcastle he said in October, 1862: "We may have our own opinions about slavery; we may be for or against the South; but there is no doubt that Jefferson Davis and other leaders of the South have made an army; they are making, it appears, a navy; and they have made, what is more than either—they have made a nation."

The Prime Minister, Lord Palmerston, wished to intervene in the American war and bring about an amicable separation into two countries, and so, apparently, did the Foreign Secretary, Lord John Russell. Recently, the American minister had vainly protested against the sailing of a ship known as 290 which was being equipped at Liverpool presumably for the service of the Confederacy, and which became the famous Alabama. For two years it roved the ocean destroying Northern commerce, and not until it was sunk at last in a battle with the U. S. S. Kearsarge did all the maritime interests of the North breathe again freely. In time and as a result of arbitration, England paid for the ships sunk by the Alabama. But in 1862, the protests of the American minister fell on deaf ears.

It must be added that the sailing of the Alabama from Liverpool was due probably to the carelessness of British officials rather than to deliberate purpose. And yet the fact is clear that about the first of October, 1862, the British ministry was on the verge of intervening to secure recognition of the independence of the Southern confederacy. The chief motive pressing them forward was the distress in England caused by the lack of cotton which resulted from the American blockade. In 1860, the South had exported 615,000 bales; in 1861, only 10,127 bales. In 1862 half the spindles of Manchester were idle; the workmen were out of employment; the owners were without dividends. It was chiefly by these manufacturing capitalists that pressure was put upon the ministry, and it was in the manufacturing district that Gladstone, thinking the Government was likely to intervene, made his allusion to the South as a nation.

Meanwhile the Emperor of the French was considering a proposal to England and Russia to join with him in mediation between the American belligerents. On October 28, 1862, Napoleon III gave audience to the Confederate envoy at Paris, discussed the Southern cause in the most friendly manner, questioned him upon the Maryland campaign, plainly indicated his purpose to attempt intervention, and at parting cordially shook hands with him. Within a few days the Emperor made good his implied promise.

The month of November, 1862, is one of the turningpoints in American foreign relations. Both Russia and England rejected France's proposal. The motive usually assigned to the Emperor Alexander is his hatred of everything associated with slavery. His own most famous action was the liberation of the Russian serfs. The motives of the British ministry, however, appear more problematical.

Mr. Rhodes thinks he can discern evidence that Adams communicated indirectly to Palmerston the contents of a dispatch from Seward which indicated that the United States would accept war rather than mediation. Palmerston had kept his eyes upon the Maryland campaign, and Lee's withdrawal did not increase his confidence in the strength of the South. Lord Russell, two months previous, had flatly told the Confederate envoy at London that the South need not hope for recognition unless it could establish itself without aid, and that "the fluctuating events of the war, the alternation of defeat and victory," composed such a contradictory situation that "Her Majesty's Government are still determined to wait."

Perhaps the veiled American warning—assuming it was conveyed to Palmerston, which seems highly probable—was not the only diplomatic innuendo of the autumn of 1862 that has escaped the pages of history. Slidell at Paris, putting together the statements of the British Ambassador and those of the French Minister of Foreign Affairs, found in them contradictions as to what was going on between the two governments in relation to America. He took a hand by attempting to inspire M. Drouyn de L'huys with distrust of England, telling him he "HAD SEEN . . . a letter from a leading member of the British Cabinet . . . in which he very plainly insinuated that France was playing an unfair game," trying to use England as Napoleon's catspaw. Among the many motives that may well have animated the Palmerston Government in its waiting policy, a distrust of Napoleon deserves to be considered.

It is scarcely rash, however, to find the chief motive in home politics. The impetuous Gladstone at Newcastle lost his head and spoke too soon. The most serious effect of his premature utterance was the prompt reaction of the "Northern party" in the Cabinet and in the country. Whatever Palmerston's secret desires were, he was not prepared to take the high hand, and he therefore permitted other members of the Cabinet to state in public that Gladstone had been misunderstood. In an interview with Adams, Lord Russell, "whilst endeavoring to excuse Mr. Gladstone," assured him that "the policy of the Government was to adhere to a strict neutrality and leave the struggle to settle itself." In the last analysis, the Northern party in England was gaining ground. The news from America, possibly, and Gladstone's rashness, certainly, roused it to increased activity. Palmerston, whose tenure of power was none too secure, dared not risk a break that might carry the disaffected into the ranks of the Opposition.

From this time forward the North rapidly grew in favor in British public opinion, and its influence upon the Government speedily increased.

Says Lord Charnwood in his recent life of Lincoln: "The battle of Antietam was followed within five days by an event which made it impossible for any government of this country to take action unfriendly to the North." He refers of course to the Emancipation Proclamation, which was issued on September 23, 1862. Lord Charnwood's remark may be too dramatic. But there can be no doubt that the Emancipation Proclamation was the turning-point in Lincoln's foreign policy; and because of it, his friends in England eventually forced the Government to play into his hands, and so frustrated Napoleon's scheme for intervention. Consequently Lincoln was able to maintain the blockade by means of which the South was strangled. Thus, at bottom, the crucial matter was Emancipation.

Lincoln's policy with regard to slavery passed through three distinct stages. As we have seen, he proposed, at first, to pledge the Government not to interfere with slavery in the States where it then existed. This was his maximum of compromise. He would not agree to permitting its extension into new territory. He maintained this position through 1861, when it was made an accusation against him by the Abolitionists and contributed to the ebb of his popularity. It also played a great part in the episode of Fremont. At a crucial moment in Fremont's career, when his hold upon popularity seemed precarious, he set at naught the policy of the President and issued an order (August 30, 1861), which confiscated all property and slaves of those who were in arms against the United States or actively aiding the enemy, and which created a "bureau of abolition." Whether Fremont was acting from conviction or "playing politics" may be left to his biographers. In a most tactful letter Lincoln asked him to modify the order so as to conform to the Confiscation Act of Congress; and when Fremont proved obdurate, Lincoln ordered him to do so. In the outcry against

Lincoln when Fremont was at last removed, the Abolitionists rang the changes on this reversal of his policy of military abolition.

Another Federal General, Benjamin F. Butler, in the course of 1861, also raised the issue, though not in the bold fashion of Fremont. Runaway slaves came to his camp on the Virginia coast, and he refused to surrender them to the owners. He took the ground that, as they had probably been used in building Confederate fortifications, they might be considered contraband of war. He was sustained by Congress, which passed what is commonly called the First Confiscation Act providing that slaves used by Confederate armies in military labor should, if captured, be "forfeited"—which of course meant that they should be set free. But this did not settle what should be done with runaways whose masters, though residents of seceded States, were loyal to the Union. The War Department decided that they should be held until the end of the war, when probably there would be made "just compensation to loyal masters."

This first stage of Lincoln's policy rested upon the hope that the Union might be restored without prolonged war. He abandoned this hope about the end of the year. Thereupon, his policy entered its second stage. In the spring of 1862 he formulated a plan for gradual emancipation with compensation. The slaves of Maryland, Delaware, Kentucky, Missouri, and the District of Columbia were to be purchased at the rate of $400 each, thus involving a total expenditure of $173,000,000. Although Congress adopted the joint resolution recommended by the President, the "border States" would not accept the plan. But Congress, by virtue of its plenary power, freed the slaves by purchase in the District of Columbia, and prohibited slavery in all the territories of the United States.

During the second stage of his policy Lincoln again had to reverse the action of an unruly general. The Federal forces operating from their base at Port Royal had occupied a considerable portion of the Carolina coast. General Hunter issued an order freeing all the slaves in South Carolina, Georgia, and Florida. In countermanding the order, Lincoln made another futile appeal to the people of the border States to adopt some plan of compensated emancipation.

"I do not argue," he said; "I beseech you to make arguments for yourselves. You cannot, if you would be blind to the signs of the times. I beg of you a calm and enlarged consideration of them, ranging, if it may be, far above personal and partisan politics. This proposal makes common cause for a common object, casting no reproaches upon any. It acts not the

Pharisee. The change it contemplates would come gently as the dews of heaven, not rending or wrecking anything. Will you not embrace it? So much good has not been done by one effort in all past time, as in the providence of God it is now your high privilege to do. May the vast future not have to lament that you neglected it. "

This persuasive attitude and reluctance to force the issue had greatly displeased the Abolitionists. Their most gifted orator, Wendell Phillips, reviled Lincoln with all the power of his literary genius, and with a fury that might be called malevolent. Meanwhile, a Second Confiscation Act proclaimed freedom for the slaves of all those who supported the Confederate Government. Horace Greeley now published in the "New York Tribune" an editorial entitled, "The Prayer of Twenty Millions." He denounced Lincoln's treatment of Fremont and Hunter and demanded radical action. Lincoln replied in a letter now famous. "I would save the Union," said he, "I would save it the shortest way under the Constitution... If I could save the Union without freeing any slave, I would do it; and if I could save it by freeing some and leaving others alone, I would also do that. What I do about slavery and the colored race, I do because I believe it helps to save the Union; and what I forbear, I forbear because I do not believe it would help to save the Union."

However, at the very time when he wrote this remarkable letter, he had in his own mind entered upon the third stage of his policy. He had even then discussed with his Cabinet an announcement favoring general emancipation. The time did not seem to them ripe. It was decided to wait until a Federal victory should save the announcement from appearing to be a cry of desperation. Antietam, which the North interpreted as a victory, gave Lincoln his opportunity.

The Emancipation Proclamation applied only to the States in arms against the Federal Government. Such States were given three months in which to return to the Union. Thereafter, if they did not return, their slaves would be regarded by that Government as free. No distinction was made between slaves owned by supporters of the Confederacy and those whose owners were in opposition to it. The Proclamation had no bearing on those slave States which had not seceded. Needless to add, no seceded State returned, and a second Proclamation making their slaves theoretically free was in due time issued on the first of January, 1863.

It must not be forgotten that this radical change of policy was made in September, 1862. We have already heard of the elections which took place soon after—those elections which mark perhaps the lowest ebb of Lincoln's popularity, when Seymour was elected Governor of New York, and the peace party gained over thirty seats in Congress. It is a question whether, as a purely domestic measure, the Emancipation Proclamation was not, for the time, an injury to the Lincoln Government. And yet it was the real turningpoint in the fortunes of the North. It was the central fact in the maintenance of the blockade.

In England at this time the cotton famine was at its height. Nearly a million people in the manufacturing districts were wholly dependent upon charity. This result of the blockade had been foreseen by the Confederate Government which was confident that the distress of England's working people would compel the English ministry to intervene and break the blockade. The employers in England whose loss was wholly financial, did as the Confederates hoped they would do. The workmen, however, took a different course. Schooled by a number of able debaters, they fell into line with that third group of political leaders who saw in the victory of the North, whatever its motives, the eventual extinction of slavery. To these people, the Emancipation Proclamation gave a definite programme. It was now, the leaders argued, no longer a question of eventual effect; the North had proclaimed a motive and that motive was the extinction of slavery. Great numbers of Englishmen of all classes who had hitherto held back from supporting Cobden and Bright now ranged themselves on their side. Addresses of praise and sympathy "began to pour into the Legation of the United States in a steady and ever swelling stream." An immense popular demonstration took place at Exeter Hall. Cobden, writing to Sumner, described the new situation in British politics, in a letter amounting to an assurance that the Government never again would attempt to resist the popular pressure in favor of the North.

On the last day of 1862 a meeting of workingmen at Manchester, where the cotton famine was causing untold misery, adopted one of those New Year greetings to Lincoln. Lincoln's reply expressed with his usual directness his own view of the sympathetic relation that had been established between the democratic classes of the two countries:

"I know and deeply deplore the sufferings which the workingmen at Manchester, and in all Europe, are called to endure in this crisis. It has been often and studiously represented that the attempt to overthrow this

Government, which was built upon the foundation of human rights, and to substitute for it one which should rest exclusively on the basis of human slavery, was likely to obtain the favor of Europe. Through the action of our disloyal citizens, the workingmen of Europe have been subjected to severe trials, for the purpose of forcing their sanction to that attempt. Under the circumstances, I cannot but regard your decisive utterances upon the question as an instance of sublime Christian heroism which has not been surpassed in any age or in any country. It is indeed an energetic and reinspiring assurance of the inherent power of truth, and of the ultimate triumph of justice, humanity, and freedom. I do not doubt that the sentiments you have expressed will be sustained by your great nation; and, on the other hand, I have no hesitation in assuring you that they will excite admiration, esteem, and the most reciprocal feelings of friendship among the American people. I hail this interchange of sentiment, therefore, as an augury that whatever else may happen, whatever misfortune may befall your country or my own, the peace and friendship which now exists between the two nations will be, as it shall be my desire to make them, perpetual."

CHAPTER X.
THE SECRETARY OF THE TREASURY

Though the defeat of the Democrats at the polls in 1863 and the now definitely friendly attitude of England had done much to secure the stability of the Lincoln Government, this success was due in part to a figure which now comes to the front and deserves attentive consideration. Indeed the work of Salmon Portland Chase, Secretary of the Treasury, forms a bridge, as one might say, between the first and second phases of Lincoln's administration.

The interesting Englishman who is the latest biographer of Lincoln says of Chase: "Unfortunately, this imposing person was a sneak." But is Lord Charnwood justified in that surprising characterization? He finds support in the testimony of Secretary Welles, who calls Chase, "artful dodger, unstable, and unreliable." And yet there is another side, for it is the conventional thing in America to call him our greatest finance minister since Hamilton, and even a conspicuous enemy said of him, at a crucial moment, that his course established his character "as an honest and frank man."

Taking these contradictory estimates as hints of a contradiction in the man, we are forced to the conclusion that Chase was a professional in politics and an amateur in finance. Perhaps herein is the whole explanation of the two characteristics of his financial policy—his reluctance to lay taxes, and his faith in loans. His two eyes did not see things alike. One was really trying to make out the orthodox path of finance; the other was peering along the more devious road of popular caprice.

The opening of the war caught the Treasury, as it caught all branches of the Government, utterly unprepared. Between April and July, 1861, Chase had to borrow what he could. When Congress met in July, his real career as director of financial policy began—or, as his enemies think, failed to begin. At least, he failed to urge upon Congress the need of new taxes and appeared satisfied with himself asking for an issue of $240,000,000 in bonds bearing not less than seven per cent interest. Congress voted to give him $250,000,000 of which $50,000,000 might be interest-bearing treasury notes; made slight increases in duties; and Prepared for excise and direct taxation the following year. Later in the year Congress laid a three per cent tax on all incomes in excess of $800.

When Congress reassembled in December, 1861, expenditures were racing ahead of receipts, and there was a deficit of $143,000,000. It must not be forgotten that this month was a time of intense excitability and of nervous reaction. Fremont had lately been removed, and the attack on Cameron had begun. At this crucial moment the situation was made still more alarming by the action of the New York banks, followed by all other banks, in suspending specie payments. They laid the responsibility upon Chase. A syndicate of banks in New York, Boston, and Philadelphia had come to the aid of the Government, but when they took up government bonds, Chase had required them to pay the full value cash down, though they had asked permission to hold the money on deposit and to pay it as needed on requisition by the Government. Furthermore, in spite of their protest, Chase issued treasury notes, which the banks had to receive from their depositors, who nevertheless continued to demand specie. On January 1, 1862, the banks owed $459,000,000 and had in specie only $87,000,000. Chase defended his course by saying that the financial crisis was not due to his policy—or lack of policy, as it would now seem—but to a general loss of faith in the outcome of the war.

There now arose a moral crisis for this "imposing person" who was Secretary of the Treasury—a crisis with regard to which there are still differences of opinion. While he faced his problem silently, the Committee on Ways and Means in the House took the matter in hand: Its solution was an old one which all sound theorists on finance unite in condemning—the issue of irredeemable paper money. And what did the Secretary of the Treasury do? Previously, as Governor of Ohio, he had denounced paper money as, in effect, a fraud upon society. Long after, when the tide of fortune had landed him in the high place of Supreme Justice, he returned to this view and condemned as unconstitutional the law of 1862 establishing a system of paper money. But at the time when that law was passed Chase, though he went through the form of protesting, soon acquiesced. Before long he was asking Congress to allow a further issue of what he had previously called "fraudulent" money.

The answer to the question whether Chase should have stuck to his principles and resigned rather than acquiesce in the paper money legislation turns on that other question—how were the politician and the financier related in his make-up?

Before Congress and the Secretary had finished, $450,000,000 were issued. Prices naturally rose, and there was speculation in gold. Even before the first issue of paper money, the treasury notes had been slightly below par. In January, 1863, a hundred dollars in paper would bring, in New York, only $69.00 in gold; a year later, after falling, rising, and falling again, the value was $64.00; in July and August, 1864, it was at its lowest, $39.00; when the war closed, it had risen to $67.00. There was powerful protest against the legislation responsible for such a condition of affairs. Justin Morrill, the author of the Morrill tariff, said, "I would as soon provide Chinese wooden guns for the army as paper money alone for the army. It will be a breach of public faith. It will injure creditors; it will increase prices; it will increase many fold the cost of the war." Recent students agree, in the main, that his prophecies were fulfilled; and a common estimate of the probable increase in the cost of the war through the use of paper money and the consequent inflation of prices is $600,000,000.

There was much more financial legislation in 1862; but Chase continued to stand aside and allow Congress the lead in establishing an excise law, an increase in the income tax, and a higher tariff—the last of which was necessitated by the excise law which has been described as a bill "that taxed everything." To enable American manufacturers to bear the excise duties levied upon their business, protection was evoked to secure them the possession of their field by excluding foreign competition. All these taxes, however, produced but a fraction of the Government's revenue. Borrowing, the favorite method of the Secretary, was accepted by Congress as the main resource. It is computed that by means of taxation there was raised in the course of the war $667,163,247.00, while during the same period the Government borrowed $2,621,916,786.00.

Whatever else he may think of Chase, no one denies that in 1862 he had other interests besides finance. Lincoln's Cabinet in those days was far from an harmonious body. All through its history there was a Chase faction and a Seward faction. The former had behind them the Radical Republicans, while the latter relied upon the support of the moderates. This division in the Republican party runs deep through the politics of the time. There seems to be good reason to think that Chase was not taken by surprise when his radical allies in Congress, in December, 1862, demanded of Lincoln the removal of Seward. It will be remembered that the elections of the autumn of 1862 had gone against Lincoln. At this moment of dismay, the friends of Chase struck their blow. Seward instantly offered his resignation. But Lincoln skillfully temporized. Thereupon, Chase also resigned. Judging from the scanty evidence we have of his intention, we may conclude that he thought he had Lincoln in a corner and that he expected either to become first minister or the avowed chief of an irresistible opposition. But he seems to have gone too fast for his followers. Lincoln had met them, together with his Cabinet, in a conference in December, 1862, and frankly discussed the situation, with the result that some of them wavered. When Lincoln informed both Seward and Chase that he declined to accept their resignations, both returned—Seward with alacrity, Chase with reluctance. One of the clues to Lincoln's cabinet policy was his determination to keep both these factions committed to the Government, without allowing himself to be under the thumb of either.

During the six months following the cabinet crisis Chase appears at his best. A stupendous difficulty lay before him and he attacked it manfully. The Government's deficit was $276,900,000. Of the loans authorized in 1862—the "five-twenties" as they were called, bringing six per cent and to run from five to twenty years at the Government's pleasure—-the sales had brought in, to December, 1862, only $23,750,000, though five hundred million had been expected. The banks in declining to handle these bonds laid the blame on the Secretary, who had insisted that all purchasers should take them at par.

It is not feasible, in a work of this character, to enter into the complexities of the financial situation of 1863, or to determine just what influences caused a revolution in the market for government bonds. But two factors must be mentioned. Chase was induced to change his attitude and to sell to banks large numbers of bonds at a rate below par, thus enabling the banks to dispose of them at a profit. He also called to his aid Jay Cooke, an experienced banker, who was allowed a commission of one-half per cent on all bonds sold up to $10,000,000 and three-eighths of one per cent after that. Cooke organized a countrywide agency system, with twenty-five hundred subagents through whom he offered directly to the people bonds in small denominations. By all manner of devices, patriotism and the purchase of bonds were made to appear the same thing, and before the end of the year $400,000,000 in five-twenty bonds had been sold. This campaign to dispose of the five-twenties was the turning-point in war finance, and later borrowings encountered no such difficulties as those of 1862 and 1863.

Better known today than this precarious legislation is the famous Act of 1863, which was amended in the next year and which forms the basis of our present system of national banks. To Chase himself the credit for this seems to be due. Even in 1861 he advised Congress to establish a system of national banks, and he repeated the advice before it was finally taken. The central feature of this system which he advocated is one with which we are still familiar: permission to the banks accepting government supervision to deposit government bonds in the Treasury and to acquire in return the right to issue bank-notes to the amount of ninety per cent of the value of the bonds.

There can be no doubt that Chase himself rated very highly his own services to his country. Nor is there any doubt that, alone among Lincoln's close associates, he continued until the end to believe himself a better man than the President. He and his radical following made no change in their attitude to Lincoln, though Chase pursued a course of confidential criticism which has since inspired the characterization of him as a "sneak," while his followers were more outspoken. In the summer of 1863 Chase was seriously talked of as the next President, and before the end of the year Chase clubs were being organized in all the large cities to promote his candidacy. Chase himself took the adroit position of not believing that any President should serve a second term.

Early in 1864 the Chase organization sent out a confidential circular signed by Senator Pomeroy of Kansas setting forth the case against Lincoln as a candidate and the case in favor of Chase. Unfortunately for Chase, this circular fell into the hands of a newspaper and was published. Chase at once wrote to Lincoln denying any knowledge of the circular but admitting his candidacy and offering his resignation. No more remarkable letter was written by Lincoln than his reply to Chase, in which he showed that he had long fully understood the situation, and which he closed with these words: "Whether you shall remain at the head of the Treasury Department is a question which I do not allow myself to consider from any standpoint other than my judgment of the public service, and, in that view, I do not perceive occasion for change."

The Chase boom rapidly declined. The deathblow was given by a caucus of the Union members of the legislature of his own State nominating Lincoln "at the demand of the people and the soldiers of Ohio." The defeat embittered Chase. For several months, however, he continued in the Cabinet, and during this time he had the mortification of seeing Lincoln renominated in the National Union Convention amid a great display of enthusiasm.

More than once in the past, Chase had offered his resignation. On one occasion Lincoln had gone to his house and had begged him to reconsider his decision. Soon after the renomination, Chase again offered his resignation upon the pretext of a disagreement with the President over appointments to office. This time, however, Lincoln felt the end had come and accepted the resignation. Chase's successor in the Treasury was William Pitt Fessenden, Senator from Maine. During most of the summer of 1864 Chase stood aside, sullen and envious, watching the progress of Lincoln toward a second election. So much did his bitterness affect his judgment that he was capable of writing in his diary his belief that Lincoln meant to reverse his policy and consent to peace with slavery reestablished.

CHAPTER XI.
NORTHERN LIFE DURING THE WAR

The real effects of war on the life of nations is one of those old and complicated debates which lie outside the scope of a volume such as this. Yet in the particular case of the Northern people it is imperative to answer two questions both of which have provoked interminable discussion: Was the moral life of the North good or bad in the war years? Was its commercial life sound?

As to the moral question, contemporary evidence seems at first sight contradictory. The very able Englishman who represented the "Times", William H. Russell, gives this ugly picture of an American city in 1863:

> "Every fresh bulletin from the battlefield of Chickamauga, during my three weeks' stay in Cincinnati, brought a long list of the dead and wounded of the Western army, many of whom, of the officers, belonged to the best families of the place. Yet the signs of mourning were hardly anywhere perceptible; the noisy gaiety of the town was not abated one jot."

On the other hand, a private manuscript of a Cincinnati family describes the "intense gloom hanging over the city like a pall" during the period of that dreadful battle. The memories of old people at Cincinnati in after days—if they had belonged to the "loyal" party—contained only sad impressions of a city that was one great hospital where "all our best people" worked passionately as volunteer assistants of the government medical corps.

A third fact to be borne in mind in connection with this apparent contradiction in evidence is the source of the greater fortunes of Cincinnati, a large proportion of which are to be traced, directly or indirectly to government contracts during the war. In some cases the merciless indifference of the Cincinnati speculators to the troubles of their country are a local scandal to this day, and it is still told, sometimes with scorn, sometimes with amusement, how perhaps the greatest of these fortunes was made by forcing up the price of iron at a time when the Government had to have iron, cost what it might.

Thus we no sooner take up the moral problem of the times than we find ourselves involved in the commercial question, for here, as always, morals and business are intertwined. Was the commercial management of the North creditable to the Government and an honor to the people? The surest way to answer such questions is to trace out with some fullness the commercial and industrial conditions of the North during the four years of war.

The general reader who looks for the first time into the matter is likely to be staggered by what statistics seem to say. Apparently they contradict what he is accustomed to hear from popular economists about the waste of war. He has been told in the newspapers that business is undermined by the withdrawal of great numbers of men from "productive" consumption of the fruits of labor and their engagement as soldiers in "unproductive" consumption. But, to his astonishment, he finds that the statistics of 1861-1865 show much increase in Northern business —as, for example, in 1865, the production of 142 million pounds of wool against 60 million in 1860. The government reports show that 13 million tons of coal were mined in 1860 and 21 million in 1864; in 1860, the output of pig iron was 821,000 tons, and 1,014,282 tons in 1864; the petroleum production rose from 21 million gallons in 1860 to 128 million in 1862; the export of corn, measured in money, shows for 1860 a business of $2,399,808 compared with $10,592,704 for 1863; wheat exporting showed, also, an enormous increase, rising from 14 millions in 1860 to 46 millions in 1863. There are, to be sure, many statistics which seem to contradict these. Some of them will be mentioned presently. And yet, on the whole, it seems safe to conclude that the North, at the close of the third year of war was producing more and was receiving larger profits than in 1860.

To deal with this subject in its entirety would lead us into the labyrinths of complex economic theory, yet two or three simple facts appear so plain that even the mere historian may venture to set them forth. When we look into the statistics which seem to show a general increase of business during the war, we find that in point of fact this increase was highly specialized. All those industries that dealt with the physical necessities of life and all those that dealt peculiarly with armies flourished amazingly. And yet there is another side to the story, for there were other industries that were set back and some that almost, if not entirely, disappeared. A good instance is the manufacture of cotton cloth. When the war opened, 200,000 hands were employed in this manufacture in New England. With the sealing up of the South and the failure of the cotton supply, their work temporarily ceased. What became of the workmen? Briefly, one of three things happened: some went into other trades, such as munitions, in which the war had created an abnormal demand for labor; a great number of them became soldiers; and many of them went West and became farmers or miners. Furthermore, many whose trades were not injured by the war left their jobs and fled westward to escape conscription. Their places were left open to be filled by operatives from the injured trades. In one or another of these ways the laborer who was thrown out of work was generally able to recover employment. But it is important to remember that the key to the labor situation at that time was the vast area of unoccupied land which could be had for nothing or next to nothing. This fact is brought home by a comparison of the situation of the American with that of the English workman during the cotton famine. According to its own ideas England was then fully cultivated. There was no body of land waiting to be thrown open, as an emergency device, to a host of new-made agriculturists. When the cotton-mills stopped at Manchester, their operatives had practically no openings but in other industrial occupations. As such opportunities were lacking, they became objects of charity until they could resume their work. As a country with a great reserve of unoccupied land, the United States was singularly fortunate at this economic crisis.

One of the noteworthy features of Northern life during the war is that there was no abnormal increase in pauperism. A great deal has been written upon the extensive charities of the time, but the term is wrongly applied, for what is really referred to is the volunteer aid given to the Government in supporting the armies. This was done on a vast scale, by all classes of the population—that is, by all who supported the Union party, for the separation between the two parties was bitter and unforgiving. But of charity in the ordinary sense of the care of the destitute there was no significant increase because there was no peculiar need. Here again the fact that the free land could be easily reached is the final explanation. There was no need for the unemployed workman to become a pauper. He could take advantage of the Homestead Act[19], which was passed in 1862, and acquire a farm of 160 acres free; or he could secure at almost nominal cost farm-land which had been given to railways as an inducement to build. Under the Homestead Act, the Government gave away land amounting to 2,400,000 acres before the close of the war. The Illinois Central alone sold to actual settlers 221,000 acres in 1863 and 264,000 in 1864. It was during the war, too, that the great undertaking of the transcontinental railway was begun, partly for military and partly for commercial reasons. In this project, both as a field of labor and as a stimulus to Western settlement, there is also to be found one more device for the relief of the labor situation in the East.

There is no more important phenomenon of the time than the shifting of large masses of population from the East to the West, while the war was in progress. This fact begins to indicate why there was no shortage in the agricultural output. The North suffered acutely from inflation of prices and from a speculative wildness that accompanied the inflation, but it did not suffer from a lack of those things that are produced by the soil—food, timber, metals, and coal. In addition to the reason just mentioned—the search for new occupation by Eastern labor which had been thrown out of employment—three other causes helped to maintain the efficiency of work in the mines, in the forests, and on the farms. These three factors were immigration, the labor of women, and labor-saving machines.

Immigration, naturally, fell off to a certain degree but it did not become altogether negligible. It is probable that 110,000 able-bodied men came into the country while war was in progress—a poor offset to the many hundred thousand who became soldiers, but nevertheless a contribution that counted for something.

Vastly more important, in the work of the North, was the part taken by women. A pathetic detail with which in our own experience the world has again become familiar was the absence of young men throughout most of

---

[19] This Act, which may be regarded as the culmination of the long battle of the Northern dreamers to win "land for the landless," provided that every settler who was, or intended to be, a citizen might secure 180 acres of government land by living on it and cultivating it for five years.

the North, and the presence of women new to the work in many occupations, especially farming. A single quotation from a home missionary in Iowa tells the whole story:

"I will mention that I met more women driving teams on the road and saw more at work in the fields than men. They seem to have said to their husbands in the language of a favorite song,

'Just take your gun and go; For Ruth can drive the oxen, John, And I can use the hoe!'

"I went first to Clarinda, and the town seemed deserted. Upon inquiry for former friends, the frequent answer was, "In the army." From Hawleyville almost all the thoroughly loyal male inhabitants had gone; and in one township beyond, where I formerly preached, there are but seven men left, and at Quincy, the county seat of Adams County, but five."

Even more important than the change in the personnel of labor were the new machines of the day. During the fifteen years previous to the war American ingenuity had reached a high point. Such inventions as the sewing machine and the horse-reaper date in their practical forms from that period, and both of these helped the North to fight the war. Their further improvement, and the extension of the principles involved to many new forms of machinery, sprang from the pressing need to make up for the loss of men who were drained by the army from the farms and the workshops. It was the horse-reaper, the horse-rake, the horse-thresher that enabled women and boys to work the farms while husbands, fathers, and elder brothers were at the front.

All these causes maintained Northern farming at a high pitch of productivity. This efficiency is implied in some of the figures already quoted, but many others could be cited. For example, in 1859, the total production of wheat for the whole country was 173 million bushels; in 1862, the North alone produced 177 millions; even in 1864, with over a million men under arms, it still produced 160 million bushels.

It must be remembered that the great Northern army produced nothing while it consumed the products of agriculture and manufacture—food, clothing, arms, ammunition, cannon, wagons, horses, medical stores—at a rate that might have led a poetical person to imagine the army as a devouring dragon. Who, in the last analysis, provided all these supplies? Who paid the soldiers? Who supplemented their meager pay and supported their families? The people, of course; and they did so both directly and indirectly. In taxes and loans they paid to the Government about three thousand millions of dollars. Their indirect assistance was perhaps as great, though it is impossible today to estimate with any approach to accuracy the amount either in money or service. Among obvious items are the collections made by the Sanitary Commission for the benefit of the hospital service, amounting to twenty-five million dollars, and about six millions raised by the Christian Commission. In a hundred other ways both individuals and localities strained their resources to supplement those of the Government. Immense subscription lists were circulated to raise funds for the families of soldiers. The city of Philadelphia alone spent in this way in a single year $600,000. There is also evidence of a vast amount of unrecorded relief of needy families by the neighbors, and in the farming districts, such assistance, particularly in the form of fuel during winter, was very generally given.

What made possible this enormous total of contributions was, in a word, the general willingness of those supporting the war to forego luxuries. They ceased buying a great multitude of unnecessary things. But what became of the labor that had previously supplied the demand for luxuries? A part of it went the way of all other Northern labor—into new trades, into the army, or to the West—and a part continued to manufacture luxuries: for their market, though curtailed, was not destroyed. There were, indeed, two populations in the North, and they were separated by an emotional chasm. Had all the North been a unit in feeling, the production of articles of luxury might have ceased. Because of this emotional division of the North, however, this business survived; for the sacrifice of luxurious expenditure was made by only a part of the population, even though it was the majority.

Furthermore, the whole matter was adjusted voluntarily without systematic government direction, since there was nothing in the financial policy of the Government to correspond to conscription. Consequently, both in the way of loans and in the way of contributions, as well as in the matter of unpaid service, the entire burden fell upon the war party alone. In the absence of anything like economic conscription, if such a phrase may be used, those Northerners who did not wish to lend money, or to make financial sacrifice, or to give unpaid service, were free to pursue their own bent. The election of 1864 showed that they formed a market which amounted to something between six and nine millions. There is no reason to suppose that these millions in 1864 spent less on luxuries than they did in 1860. Two or three items are enough. In 1860, the importation of silk amounted to 32 million dollars; in 1862, in spite of inflated prices, it had shrunk to 7 millions; the consumption of malt liquors shrank from 101 million gallons in 1860 to 62 million gallons in 1863; of coffee, hardly to be classed as a luxury, there were consumed in 1861, 184 million pounds and in 1863, 80 millions.

The clue to the story of capital is to be found in this fact, too often forgotten, that there was an economic-political division cutting deep through every stratum of the Northern people. Their economic life as well as their political life was controlled on the one hand by a devotion to the cause of the war, and on the other hand by a hatred of that cause or by cynical indifference. And we cannot insist too positively that the Government failed very largely to take this fact into account. The American spirit of invention, so conspicuous at that time in mechanics, did not apply itself to the science of government. Lincoln confessedly was not a financier; his instinct was at home only in problems that could be stated in terms of men. Witness his acceptance of conscription and his firmness in carrying it through, as a result of which he saved the patriotic party from bearing the whole burden of military service. But there was no parallel conservation of power in the field of industry. The financial policy, left in the hands of Chase, may truly be described as barren of ideas. Incidentally, it may be mentioned that the "loyal" North was left at the mercy of its domestic enemies and a prey to parasites by Chase's policy of loans instead of taxes and of voluntary support instead of enforced support.

The consequence of this financial policy was an immense opportunity for the "disloyally" and the parasites to make huge war profits out of the "loyals" and the Government. Of course, it must not be supposed that everyone who seized the chance to feather his nest was so careless or so impolitic as to let himself be classed as a "disloyal." An incident of the autumn of 1861 shows the temper of those professed "loyals" who were really parasites. The background of the incident is supplied by a report of the Quartermaster-General:

"Governors daily complain that recruiting will stop unless clothing is sent in abundance and immediately to the various recruiting camps and regiments. With every exertion, this department has not been able to obtain clothing to supply these demands, and they have been so urgent that troops before the enemy have been compelled to do picket duty in the late cold nights without overcoats, or even coats, wearing only thin summer flannel blouses . . . Could 150,000 suits of clothing, overcoats, coats, and pantaloons be placed today, in depot, it would scarce supply the calls now before us. They would certainly leave no surplus."

The Government attempted to meet this difficulty in the shortest possible time by purchasing clothing abroad. But such disregard of home industry, the "patriotism" of the New England manufacturers could not endure. Along with the report just quoted, the Quartermaster-General forwarded to the Secretary of War a long argumentative protest from a committee of the Boston Board of Trade against the purchase of army clothing in Europe. Any American of the present day can guess how the protest was worded and what arguments were used. Stripped of its insincerity, it signified this: the cotton mills were inoperative for lack of material; their owners saw no chance to save their dividends except by requipment as woolen mills; the existing woolen mills also saw a great chance to force wool upon the market as a substitute for cotton. In Ohio, California, Pennsylvania, and Illinois, the growers of wool saw the opportunity with equal clearness. But, one and all, these various groups of parasites saw that their game hinged on one condition: the munitions market must be kept open until they were ready to monopolize government contracts. If soldiers contracted pneumonia doing picket duty on cold nights, in their summer blouses, that was but an unfortunate incident of war.

Very different in spirit from the protest of the Boston manufacturers is a dispatch from the American minister at Brussels which shows what American public servants, in contrast with American manufacturers, were about. Abroad the agents of North and South were fighting a commercial duel in which each strove to monopolize the munitions market. The United States Navy, seeing things from an angle entirely different from that of the Boston Board of Trade, ably seconded the ministers by blockading the Southern ports and by thus preventing the movement of specie and cotton to Europe. As a consequence, fourmonth notes which had been given by Southern agents with their orders fell due, had to be renewed, and began to be held in disfavor. Agents of the North, getting wind of these hitches in negotiations, eagerly sought to take over the unpaid Confederate orders. All these details of the situation help to explain the jubilant tone of this dispatch from Brussels late in November, 1861:

"I have now in my hands complete control of the principal rebel contracts on the continent, viz.: 206,000 yards of cloth ready for delivery, already commencing to move forward to Havre; gray but can be dyed blue in twenty days; 100,000 yards deliverable from 15th of December to 26th of January, light blue army cloth, same as ours; 100,000 blankets; 40,000 guns to be shipped in ten days; 20,000 saber bayonets to be delivered in six weeks . . . The winter clothing for 100,000 men taken out of their hands, when they cannot replace it, would almost compensate for Bull Run. There is no considerable amount of cloth to be had in Europe; the stocks are very short."

The Secretary of War was as devoid of ideas as the Secretary of the Treasury was and even less equipped with resisting power. Though he could not undo the work already done by the agents of the Government abroad, he gave way as rapidly as possible to the allied parasites whose headquarters, at the moment, were in Boston. The story grows uglier as we proceed. Two powerful commercial combinations took charge of the policy of the woolen interests—the National Woolgrowers' Association and the National Association of Wool Manufacturers, which were soon in control of this immense industry. Woolen mills sprang up so fast that a report of the New York Chamber of Commerce pronounced their increase "scarcely credible." So great was the new market created by the Government demand, and so ruthless were the parasites in forcing up prices, that dividends on mill stock rose to 10, 15, 25, and even 40 per cent. And all the while the wool growers and the wool manufacturers were clamoring to Congress for protection of the home industry, exclusion of the wicked foreign competition, and all in the name of their devoted "patriotism"—patriotism with a dividend of 40 per cent!

Of course, it is not meant that every wool grower and every woolen manufacturer was either a "disloyal" or a parasite. By no means. Numbers of them were to be found in that great host of "loyals" who put their dividends into government bonds and gave their services unpaid as auxiliaries of the Commissary Department or the Hospital Service of the Army. What is meant is that the abnormal conditions of industry, uncorrected by the Government, afforded a glaring opportunity for unscrupulous men of business who, whatever their professions, cared a hundred times more for themselves than for their country. To these was due the pitiless hampering of the army in the interest of the wool-trade. For example, many uniforms paid for at outrageous prices, turned out to be made of a miserable cheap fabric, called "shoddy," which resisted weather scarcely better than paper. This fraud gave the word "shoddy" its present significance in our American speech and produced the phrase—applied to manufacturers newly become rich—"shoddy aristocracy." An even more shameful result of the selfishness of the manufacturers and of the weakness of the Government was the use of cloth for uniforms not of the regulation colors, with the result that soldiers sometimes fired upon their comrades by mistake.

The prosperity of the capitalists who financed the woolen business did not extend to the labor employed in it. One of the ugliest details of the time was the resolute attempt of the parasites to seize the whole amount of the abnormal profits they wrung from the Government and from the people. For it must not be forgotten that the whole nation had to pay their prices. It is estimated that prices in the main advanced about 100 per cent while wages were not advanced more than sixty per cent. It is not strange that these years of war form a period of bitter antagonism between labor and capital.

What went on in the woolen business is to be found more or less in every business. Immense fortunes sprang up over night. They had but two roots: government contracts and excessive profits due to war prices. The gigantic fortunes which characterized the North at the end of the war are thus accounted for. The so-called prosperity of the time was a class prosperity and was absorbed by parasites who fattened upon the necessities of the Government and the sacrifices of the people.

CHAPTER XII.
THE MEXICAN EPISODE

That French demagogue whom Victor Hugo aptly called Napoleon the Little was a prime factor in the history of the Union and the Confederacy. The Confederate side of his intrigue will be told in its proper place. Here, let us observe him from the point of view of Washington.

It is too much to attempt to pack into a sentence or two the complicated drama of deceit, lies, and graft, through which he created at last a pretext for intervention in the affairs of Mexico; it is enough that in the autumn of 1862 a French army of invasion marched from Vera Cruz upon Mexico City. We have already seen that about this same time Napoleon proposed to England and Russia a joint intervention with France between North and South—a proposal which, however, was rejected. This Mexican venture explains why the plan was suggested at that particular time.

Disappointed in England and Russia, Napoleon unexpectedly received encouragement, as he thought, from within the United States through the medium of the eccentric editor of the "New York Tribune". We shall have occasion to return later to the adventures of Horace Greeley—that erratic individual who has many good and generous acts to his credit, as well as many foolish ones. For the present we have to note that toward the close of 1862 he approached the French Ambassador at Washington with a request for imperial mediation between the North and the South. Greeley was a type of American that no European can understand: he believed in talk, and more talk, and still more talk, as the cure for earthly ills. He never could understand that anybody besides himself could have strong convictions. When he told the Ambassador that the Emperor's mediation would lead to a reconciliation of the sections, he was doubtless sincere in his belief. The astute European diplomat, who could not believe such simplicity, thought it a mask. When he asked for, and received, permission to pass the Federal lines and visit Richmond, he interpreted the permit in the light of his assumption about Greeley. At Richmond, he found no desire for reunion. Putting this and that together, he concluded that the North wanted to give up the fight and would welcome mediation to save its face. The dreadful defeat at Fredericksburg fell in with this reasoning. His reports on American conditions led Napoleon, in January, 1863, to attempt alone what he had once hoped to do supported by England and Russia. He proposed his good offices to the Government at Washington as a mediator between North and South.

Hitherto, Washington had been very discreet about Mexico. Adroit hints not to go too far had been given Napoleon in full measure, but there was no real protest. The State Department now continued this caution and in the most polite terms declined Napoleon's offer. Congress, however, took the matter more grimly, for throughout the dealings with Napoleon, it had been at odds with Lincoln. It now passed the first of a series of resolutions which expressed the will of the country, if not quite the will of the President, by resolving that any further proposal of mediation would be regarded by it as "an unfriendly act."

Napoleon then resumed his scheming for joint intervention, while in the meantime his armies continued to fight their way until they entered Mexico City in June, 1863. The time had now come when Napoleon thought it opportune to show his hand. Those were the days when Lee appeared invincible, and when Chancellorsville crowned a splendid series of triumphs. In England, the Southern party made a fresh start; and societies were organized to aid the Confederacy. At Liverpool, Laird Brothers were building, ostensibly for France, really for the Confederacy, two ironclads supposed to outclass every ship in the Northern navy. In France, 100,000 unemployed cotton hands were rioting for food. To raise funds for the Confederacy the great Erlanger banking-house of Paris negotiated a loan based on cotton which was to be delivered after the breaking of the blockade. Napoleon dreamed of a shattered American union, two enfeebled republics, and a broad way for his own scheme in Mexico.

In June an English politician of Southern sympathies, Edward Roebuck, went over to France, was received by the Emperor, and came to an understanding with him. Roebuck went home to report to the Southern party that Napoleon was ready to intervene, and that all he waited for was England's cooperation. A motion "to enter into negotiations with the Great Powers of Europe for the purpose of obtaining their cooperation in the recognition" of the Confederacy was introduced by Roebuck in the House of Commons.

The debate which followed was the last chance of the Southern party and, as events proved, the last chance of Napoleon. How completely the British ministry was now committed to the North appears in the fact that Gladstone, for the Government, opposed Roebuck's motion. John Bright attacked it in what Lord Morley calls "perhaps the most powerful and the noblest speech of his life." The Southern party was hardly resolute in their support of Roebuck and presently he withdrew his motion.

But there were still the ironclads at Liverpool. We have seen that earlier in the war, the carelessness of the British authorities had permitted the escape of ship 290, subsequently known as the Confederate commercedestroyer, Alabama. The authorities did not wish to allow a repetition of the incident. But could it be shown that the Laird ships were not really for a French purchaser? It was in the course of diplomatic conversations that Mr. Adams, speaking of the possible sailing of the ships, made a remark destined to become famous: "It would be superfluous in me to point out to your lordship that this is war." At jest, the authorities were satisfied. The ships were seized and in the end bought for the British Navy.

Again Napoleon stood alone. Not only had he failed to obtain aid from abroad, but in France itself his Mexican schemes were widely and bitterly condemned. Yet he had gone too far to recede, and what he had been aiming at all along was now revealed. An assembly of Mexican notables, convened by the general of the invaders, voted to set up an imperial government and offered the crown to Napoleon's nominee, the Archduke Maximilian of Austria.

And now the Government at Washington was faced with a complicated problem. What about the Monroe Doctrine? Did the Union dare risk war with France? Did it dare pass over without protest the establishment of monarchy on American soil by foreign arms? Between these horns of a dilemma, the Government maintained its precarious position during another year. Seward's correspondence with Paris was a masterpiece of evasion. He neither protested against the intervention of Napoleon nor acknowledged the authority of Maximilian. Apparently, both he and Lincoln were divided between fear of a French alliance with the Confederacy and fear of premature action in the North that would render Napoleon desperate. Just how far they comprehended Napoleon and his problems is an open question.

Whether really comprehending or merely trusting to its instinct, Congress took a bolder course. Two men prove the antagonists of a parliamentary duel—Charles Sumner, chairman of the Senate Committee on Foreign Relations, and Henry Winter Davis, chairman of the corresponding committee of the House. Sumner played the hand of the Administration. Fiery resolutions demanding the evacuation of Mexico or an American declaration of war were skillfully buried in the silence of Sumner's committee. But there was nevertheless one resolution that affected history: it was a ringing condemnation of the attempt to establish a monarchy in Mexico. In the House, a joint resolution which Davis submitted was passed without one dissenting vote. When it came to the Senate, Sumner buried it as he had buried earlier resolutions. None the less it went out to the world attended by the news of the unanimous vote in the House.

Shortly afterwards, the American Ambassador at Paris called upon the imperial Foreign Secretary, M. Drouyn de L'huys. News of this resolution had preceded him. He was met by the curt question, "Do you bring peace or war?" Again, the Washington Government was skillfully evasive. The Ambassador was instructed to explain that the resolution had not been inspired by the President and "the French Government would be seasonably apprized of any change of policy . . . which the President might at any future time think it proper to adopt."

There seems little doubt that Lincoln's course was very widely condemned as timid. When we come to the political campaign of 1864, we shall meet Henry Winter Davis among his most relentless personal enemies. Dissatisfaction with Lincoln's Mexican policy has not been sufficiently considered in accounting for the opposition to him, inside the war party, in 1864. To it may be traced an article in the platform of the war party, adopted in June, 1864, protesting against the establishment of monarchy "in near proximity to the United States." In the same month Maximilian entered Mexico City.

The subsequent moves of Napoleon are explained elsewhere.[20] The central fact in the story is his virtual change of attitude, in the summer of 1864. The Confederate agent at Paris complained of a growing coolness. Before the end of the summer, the Confederate Secretary of State was bitter in his denunciation of Napoleon for having deserted the South. Napoleon's puppet Maximilian refused to receive an envoy from the Confederacy. Though Washington did not formally protest against the presence of Maximilian in Mexico, it declined to recognize his Government, and that Government continued unrecognized at Washington throughout the war.

---

[20] Nathaniel W. Stephenson, "The Day of the Confederacy". (In "The Chronicles of America").

CHAPTER XIII.
THE PLEBISCITE OF 1864

Every great revolution among Anglo-Saxon people—perhaps among all people—has produced strange types of dreamers. In America, however, neither section could claim a monopoly of such types, and even the latter-day visionaries who can see everything in heaven and earth, excepting fact, had their Northern and Southern originals in the time of the great American war. Among these is a strange congregation which assembled in the spring of 1864 and which has come to be known, from its place of meeting, as the Cleveland Convention. Its coming together was the result of a loose cooperation among several minor political groups, all of which were for the Union and the war, and violently opposed to Lincoln. So far as they had a common purpose, it was to supplant Lincoln by Fremont in the next election.

The Convention was notable for the large proportion of agnostics among its members. A motion was made to amend a resolution that "the Rebellion must be put down" by adding the words "with God's assistance." This touch of piety was stormily rejected. Another group represented at Cleveland was made up of extreme abolitionists under the leadership of that brilliant but disordered genius, Wendell Phillips. He sent a letter denouncing Lincoln and pledging his support of Fremont because of the latter's "clearsighted statesmanship and rare military ability." The convention declared itself a political party, under the style of the Radical Democracy, and nominated Fremont for President.

There was another body of dreamers, still more singular, who were also bitter opponents of Lincoln. They were, however, not in favor of war. Their political machinery consisted of secret societies. As early as 1860, the Knights of the Golden Circle were active in Indiana, where they did yeoman service for Breckinridge. Later this society acquired some underground influence in other States, especially in Ohio, and did its share in bringing about the victories at the polls in the autumn of 1862, when the Democrats captured the Indiana legislature.

The most serious charge against the Golden Circle was complicity in an attempt to assassinate Oliver P. Morton, Governor of Indiana, who was fired at, one night, as he was leaving the state house. When Morton demanded an investigation of the Golden Circle, the legislature refused to sanction it. On his own authority and with Federal aid he made investigations and published a report which, if it did not actually prove treason, came dangerously near to proof. Thereafter, this society drops out of sight, and its members appear to have formed the new Order of the American Knights, which in its turn was eclipsed by the Sons of Liberty. There were several other such societies all organized on a military plan and with a great pretense of arming their members. This, however, had to be done surreptitiously. Boxes of rifles purchased in the East were shipped West labeled "Sunday-school books," and negotiations were even undertaken with the Confederacy to bring in arms by way of Canada. At a meeting of the supreme council of the Sons of Liberty, in New York, February 22, 1864, it was claimed that the order had nearly a million members, though the Government secret service considered half a million a more exact estimate.

As events subsequently proved, the societies were not as formidable as these figures would imply. Most of the men who joined them seem to have been fanciful creatures who loved secrecy for its own sake. While real men, North and South, were laying down their lives for their principles, these make-believe men were holding bombastic initiations and taking oaths such as this from the ritual of the American Knights: "I do further solemnly promise and swear, that I will ever cherish the sublime lessons which the sacred emblems of our order suggest, and will, so far as in me lies, impart those lessons to the people of the earth, where the mystic acorn falls from its parent bough, in whose visible firmament Orion, Arcturus, and the Pleiades ride in their cold resplendent glories, and where the Southern Cross dazzles the eye of degraded humanity with its coruscations of golden light, fit emblem of Truth, while it invites our sacred order to consecrate her temples in the four corners of the earth, where moral darkness reigns and despotism holds sway ... Divine essence, so help me that I fail not in my troth, lest I shall be summoned before the tribunal of the order, adjudged and condemned to certain and shameful death, while my name shall be recorded on the rolls of infamy. Amen."

The secret orders fought hard to prevent the Lincoln victory in the elections of 1863. Even before that time their leaders had talked mysteriously of another disruption of the Union and the formation of a Northwestern Confederacy in alliance with the South. The scheme was known to the Confederates, allusions to it are to be found in Southern newspapers, and even the Confederate military authorities considered it. Early in 1863, General Beauregard thought the Confederates might "get into Ohio and call upon the friends of Vallandigham to rise for his defense and support; then . . . call upon the whole Northwest to join in the movement, form a confederacy of their own, and join us by a treaty of alliance, offensive and defensive." Reliance on the support of the societies was the will-o'-the-wisp that deceived General John Morgan in his desperate attempt to carry out Beauregard's programme. Though brushed aside as a mere detail by military historians, Morgan's raid, with his force of irregular cavalry, in July, 1863, through Indiana and Ohio, was one of the most romantic episodes of the war. But it ended in his defeat and capture. While his gallant troopers rode to their destruction, the men who loved to swear by Arcturus and to gabble about the Pleiades showed the fiber to be expected of such people, and stayed snug in their beds.

But neither their own lack of hardihood nor the disasters of their Southern friends could dampen their peculiar ardor. Their hero was Vallandigham. That redoubtable person had fixed his headquarters in Canada, whence he directed his partisans in their vain attempt to elect him Governor of Ohio. Their next move was to honor him with the office of Supreme Commander of the Sons of Liberty, and now Vallandigham resolved to win the martyr's crown in very fact. In June, 1864, he prepared for the dramatic effect by carefully advertising his intention and came home. But to his great disappointment Lincoln ignored him, and the dramatic martyrdom which he had planned did not come off.

There still existed the possibility of a great uprising, and to that end arrangements were made with Southern agents in Canada. Confederate soldiers, picked men, made their way in disguise to Chicago. There the worshipers of Arcturus were to join them in a mighty multitude; the Confederate prisoners at Camp Douglas in Chicago were to be liberated; around that core of veterans, the hosts of the Pleiades were to rally. All this was to coincide with the assembling at Chicago of the Democratic national convention, in which Vallandigham was to appear. The organizers of the conspiracy dreamed that the two events might coalesce; that the convention might be stampeded by their uprising; that a great part, if not the whole, of the convention would endorse the establishment of a Northwestern Confederacy.

Alas for him who builds on the frame of mind that delights in cheap rhetoric while Rome is afire! At the moment of hazard, the Sons of Liberty showed the white feather, were full of specious words, would not act. The Confederate soldiers, indignant at this second betrayal, had to make their escape from the country.

It must not be supposed that this Democratic national convention was made up altogether of Secessionists. The peace party was still, as in the previous year, a strange complex, a mixture of all sorts and conditions. Its cohesion was not so much due to its love of peace as to its dislike of Lincoln and its hatred of his party. Vallandigham was a member of the committee on resolutions. The permanent chairman was Governor Seymour of New York. The Convention was called to order by August Belmont, a foreigner by birth, the American representative of the Rothschilds. He was the head and front of that body of Northern capital which had so long financed the South and which had always opposed the war. In opening the Convention he said: "Four years of misrule by a sectional, fanatical, and corrupt party have brought our country to the verge of ruin." In the platform Lincoln was accused of a list of crimes which it had become the habit of the peace party to charge against him. His administration was described as "four years of failure," and McClellan was nominated for President.

The Republican managers called a convention at Baltimore in June, 1864, with a view to organizing a composite Union Party in which the War Democrats were to participate. Their plan was successful. The second place on the Union ticket was accepted by a War Democrat, Andrew Johnson, of Tennessee. Lincoln was renominated, though not without opposition, and he was so keenly aware that he was not the unanimous choice of the Union Party that he permitted the fact to appear in a public utterance soon afterward. "I do not allow myself," he said, in addressing a delegation of the National Union League, "to suppose that either the

Convention or the League have concluded to decide that I am either the greatest or the best man in America, but rather they have concluded it is not best to swap horses while crossing the river, and have further concluded that I am not so poor a horse that they might not make a botch of it in trying to swap."

But the Union Party was so far from being a unit that during the summer factional quarrels developed within its ranks. All the elements that were unfriendly to Lincoln took heart from a dispute between the President and Congress with regard to reconstruction in Louisiana, over a large part of which Federal troops had established a civil government on the President's authority. As an incident in the history of reconstruction, this whole matter has its place in another volume.[21] But it also has a place in the history of the presidential campaign of 1864. Lincoln's plan of reconstruction was obnoxious to the Radicals in Congress inasmuch as it did not definitely abolish slavery in Louisiana, although it required the new Government to give its adherence to the Emancipation Proclamation. Congress passed a bill taking reconstruction out of the President's hands and definitely requiring the reconstructed States to abolish slavery. Lincoln took the position that Congress had no power over slavery in the States. When his Proclamation was thrown in his teeth, he replied, "I conceive that I may in an emergency do things on military grounds which cannot be done constitutionally by Congress." Incidentally there was a further disagreement between the President and the Radicals over negro suffrage. Though neither scheme provided for it, Lincoln would extend it, if at all, only to the exceptional negroes, while the Radicals were ready for a sweeping extension. But Lincoln refused to sign their bill and it lapsed. Thereupon Benjamin Wade of Ohio and Henry Winter Davis of Maryland issued a savage denunciation of Lincoln which has been known ever since as the "Wade-Davis Manifesto".

There was a faction in the Union Party which we may justly name the Vindictives. The "Manifesto" gave them a rallying cry. At a conference in New York they decided to compel the retirement of Lincoln and the nomination of some other candidate. For this purpose a new convention was to be called at Cincinnati in September. In the ranks of the Vindictives at this time was the impetuous editor of the "New York Tribune", Horace

---

[21] Walter L. Fleming, "The Sequel of Appomattox". In "The Chronicles of America".

Greeley. His presence there calls for some explanation. Perhaps the most singular figure of the time, he was one of the most irresponsible and yet, through his paper, one of the most influential. He had a trick of phrase which, somehow, made him appear oracular to the plain people, especially in the rural districts—the very people on whom Lincoln relied for a large part of his support. Greeley knew his power, and his mind was not large enough to carry the knowledge well. Furthermore, his was the sort of nature that relates itself to life above all through the sensibilities. Kipling speaks scornfully of people who if their "own front door is shut will swear the world is warm." They are relations in the full blood of Horace Greeley.

In July, when the breach between the President and the Vindictives was just beginning to be evident, Greeley was pursuing an adventure of his own. Among the least sensible minor incidents of the war were a number of fantastic attempts of private persons to negotiate peace. With one exception they had no historic importance. The exception is a negotiation carried on by Greeley, which seems to have been the ultimate cause of his alliance with the Vindictives.

In the middle of July, 1864, gold was selling in New York at 285. There was distress and discontent throughout the country. The horrible slaughter of the Wilderness, still fresh in everybody's mind, had put the whole Union Party into mourning. The impressionable Greeley became frantic for peace at any price. At the psychological moment word was conveyed to him that two persons in Canada held authority from the Confederacy to enter into negotiations for peace. Greeley wrote to Lincoln demanding negotiations because "our bleeding, bankrupt, almost dying country longs for peace, shudders at the prospect of fresh conscriptions, of further wholesale devastations, and of new rivers of human blood."

Lincoln consented to a negotiation but stipulated that Greeley himself should become responsible for its conduct. Though this was not what Greeley wanted for his type always prefers to tell others what to do—he sullenly accepted. He proceeded to Niagara to meet the reputed commissioners of the Confederacy. The details of the futile conference do not concern us. The Confederate agents were not empowered to treat for peace—at least not on any terms that would be considered at Washington. Their real purpose was far subtler. Appreciating the delicate balance in Northern politics, they aimed at making it appear that Lincoln was begging for terms. Lincoln, who foresaw this possible turn of events, had expressly limited Greeley to negotiations for "the integrity of the whole Union and the abandonment of slavery." Greeley chose to believe that these instructions, and not the subtlety of the Confederate agents and his own impulsiveness, were the cause of the false position in which the agents now placed him. They published an account of the episode, thus effecting an exposure which led to sharp attacks upon Greeley by the Northern press. In the bitterness of his mortification Greeley then went from one extreme to the other and joined the Vindictives.

Less than three weeks after the conference at Niagara, the "Wade-Davis Manifesto" appeared. It was communicated to the country through the columns of Greeley's paper on the 5th of August. Greeley, who so short a time before was for peace at any price, went the whole length of reaction by proclaiming that "Mr. Lincoln is already beaten ... We must have another ticket to save us from utter overthrow. If we had such a ticket as could be made by naming Grant, Butler, or Sherman for President and Farragut for Vice, we could make a fight yet."

At about this same time the chairman of the Republican national committee, who was a Lincoln man, wrote to the President that the situation was desperate. Lincoln himself is known to have made a private memorandum containing the words, "It seems extremely probable that this Administration will not be reelected." On the 1st of September, 1864, with three presidential candidates in the field, Northern politics were bewildering, and the country was shrouded in the deepest gloom. The Wilderness campaign, after slaughter unparalleled, had not in the popular mind achieved results. Sherman, in Georgia, though his losses were not as terrible as Grant's, had not yet done anything to lighten the gloom. Not even Farragut's victory in Mobile Bay, in August, far-reaching as it proved to be, reassured the North. A bitter cry for peace went up even from lovers of the Union whose hearts had failed.

Meanwhile, the brilliant strategist in Georgia was pressing his drive for political as well as for military effect. To rouse those Unionists who had lost heart was part of his purpose when he hurled his columns against Atlanta, from which Hood was driven in one of the most disastrous of Confederate defeats. On the 3rd of September Lincoln issued a proclamation appointing a day of thanksgiving for these great victories of Sherman and Farragut.

On that day, it would seem, the tide turned in Northern politics. Some historians are content with Atlanta as the explanation of all that followed;

but there are three separate events of importance that now occurred as incidents in the complicated situation. In the first place, three weeks later the radical opposition had collapsed; the plan for a new convention was abandoned; the Vindictive leaders came out in support of Lincoln. Almost simultaneously occurred the remaining two surprising events. Fremont withdrew from his candidacy in order to do his "part toward preventing the election of the Democratic candidate." And Lincoln asked for the resignation of a member of his Cabinet, Postmaster-General Montgomery Blair, who was the especial enemy of the Vindictives.

The official biographers of Lincoln[22] keep these three events separate. They hold that Blair's removal was wholly Lincoln's idea, and that from chivalrous reasons he would not abandon his friend as long as he seemed to be losing the game. The historian Rhodes writes confidently of a bargain with Fremont, holding that Blair was removed to terminate a quarrel with Fremont which dated back even to his own removal in 1861. A possible third theory turns upon Chase, whose hostility to Blair was quite equal to that of the illbalanced Fremont. It had been stimulated the previous winter by a fierce arraignment of Chase made by Blair's brother in Congress, in which Chase was bluntly accused of fraud and of making money, or allowing his friends to make money, through illicit trade in cotton. And Chase was a man of might among the Vindictives. The intrigue, however, never comes to the foreground in history, but lurks in the background thick with shadows. Once or twice among those shadows we seem to catch a glimpse of the figure of Thurlow Weed, the master-politician of the time. Taking one thing with another, we may risk the guess that somehow the two radical groups which were both relentless against Blair were led to pool their issues, and that Blair's removal was the price Lincoln paid not to one faction of radicals but to the whole unmerciful crowd.

Whatever complex of purposes lay back of the triple coincidence, the latter part of September saw a general reunion of the factions within the Union Party, followed by a swift recovery of strength. When the election came, Lincoln received an electoral vote of 212 against 21, and a popular vote of 2,330,552 against 1,835,985.

The inevitable question arises as to what was the real cause of this success. It is safe to say that the political campaign contained some adroit

---

[22] His private secretaries, John G. Nicolay and John Hay.

strategy; that Sherman was without doubt an enormous factor; that the Democrats made numerous blunders; and that the secret societies had an effect other than they intended. However, the real clue seems to be found in one sentence from a letter written by Lowell to Motley when the outlook for his party was darkest: "The mercantile classes are longing for peace, but I believe that the people are more firm than ever." Of the great, silent mass of the people, the true temper seems to be struck off in a popular poem of the time, written in response to one of the calls for more troops, a poem with refrains built on the model of this couplet:

"We're coming from the hillside, we're coming from the shore, We're coming, Father Abraham, six hundred thousand more."

CHAPTER XIV.
LINCOLN'S FINAL INTENTIONS

The victory of the Union Party in November enabled Lincoln to enjoy for a brief period of his career as President what may be thought of as a lull in the storm. He knew now that he had at last built up a firm and powerful support. With this assured, his policy, both domestic and foreign—the key to which was still the blockade—might be considered victorious at all points. There remains to be noticed, however, one event of the year 1864 which was of vital importance in maintaining the blockade.

It is a principle of international law that a belligerent must itself attend to the great task of suppressing contraband trade with its enemy. Lincoln was careful to observe this principle. Though British merchants were frankly speculating in contraband trade, he made no demand upon the British Government to relieve him of the difficulty of stopping it. England also took the legitimate position under international law and warned her merchants that, while it was none of the Government's business to prevent such trade, they practised it at their own risk, subject to well-understood penalties agreed upon among nations. The merchants nevertheless continued to take the risk, while both they and the authorities of the Confederacy thought they saw a way of minimizing the danger. Instead of shipping supplies direct to the Confederate ports they shipped them to Matamoros, in Mexico, or to the West Indies. As these ports were in neutral territory, the merchants thought their goods would be safe against capture until they left the Mexican or West Indian port on their brief concluding passage to the territory of the Confederacy. Nassau, then a petty West

India town, was the chief depot of such trade and soon became a great commercial center. To it came vast quantities of European goods which were then transferred to swift, small vessels, or "blockade-runners," which took a gambler's chance and often succeeded in eluding the Federal patrol ships and in rushing their cargoes safe into a Confederate port.

Obviously, it was a great disadvantage to the United States to allow contraband supplies to be accumulated, without interference, close to the blockaded coast, and the Lincoln Government determined to remove this disadvantage. With this end in view it evoked the principle of the continuous voyage, which indeed was not new, but which was destined to become fixed in international law by the Supreme Court of the United States. American cruisers were instructed to stop British ships sailing between the British ports of Liverpool and Nassau; they were to use the recognized international rights of visit and search; and if there was evidence that the cargo was not destined for actual consumption at Nassau, they were to bring the ship into an American port to be dealt with by an American prize court. When such arrests began, the owners clamored to the British Government, and both dealers in contraband and professional blockade-runners worked themselves into a fury because American cruisers watched British ports and searched British ships on the high seas. With regard to this matter, the British Government and the Government at Washington had their last important correspondence during the war. The United States stood firm for the idea that when goods were ultimately intended for the Confederacy, no matter how roundabout the journey, they could be considered as making a single continuous voyage and were liable to capture from the day they left Liverpool. Early in 1865, the Supreme Court of the United States fully developed the principle of continuous voyage in four celebrated cases that are now among the landmarks of international law.[23]

This was the last step in making the blockade effective. Thereafter, it slowly strangled the South. The Federal armies enormously overmatched the Southern, and from November, 1864, their continuance in the field was made sure. Grim work still lay before Lincoln, but the day of anxiety was past. In this moment of comparative ease, the aged Chief Justice Taney died, and Lincoln appointed to that high position his ungenerous rival,

---

[23] The Great war has once again led to controversy over this subject, so vital to neutral states.

Chase.

Even now Lincoln had not established himself as a leader superior to party, but he had the satisfaction, early in 1865, of seeing the ranks of the opposition begin to break. Naturally, the Thirteenth Amendment to the Constitution, abolishing slavery throughout the United States, appeared to Lincoln as in a way the consummation of his labors. When the House voted on the resolution to send this amendment to the States, several Democrats joined the government forces. Two nights afterward, speaking to a serenading party at the White House, Lincoln made a brief speech, part of which is thus reported by his secretaries: "He thought this measure was a very fitting if not an indispensable adjunct to the winding up of the great difficulty. He wished the reunion of all the States perfected, and so effected as to remove all causes of disturbance in the future; and to attain this end, it was necessary that the original disturbing cause should, if possible, be rooted out."

An event which in its full detail belongs to Confederate rather than to Union history took place soon after this. At Hampton Roads, Lincoln and Seward met Confederate commissioners who had asked for a parley—with regard to peace. Nothing came of the meeting, but the conference gave rise to a legend, false in fact and yet true in spirit, according to which Lincoln wrote on a sheet of paper the word "Union," pushed it across to Alexander H. Stephens and said, "Write under that anything you please."

This fiction expresses Lincoln's attitude toward the sinking Confederacy. On his return from Hampton Roads he submitted to his Cabinet a draft of a message which he proposed to send to Congress. He recommended the appropriation of $400,000,000 to be distributed among the slave states on condition that war cease before April 1, 1865. Not a member of the Cabinet approved. His secretary, Mr. Nicolay, writes: "The President, in evident surprise and sorrow at the want of statesmanlike liberality shown by his executive council, folded and laid away the draft of his message . . . ." With a deep sigh he added, "But you are all opposed to me, and I will not send the message."

His second inauguration passed without striking incidents. Chase, as Chief Justice, administered the oath. The second inaugural address contained words which are now famous: "With malice towards none; with charity for all; with firmness in the right, as God gives us to see the right, let us strive on to finish the work we are in; to bind up the nation's wounds; to care for him who shall have borne the battle, and for his widow, and his orphan—to do all which may achieve and cherish a just and a lasting peace among ourselves, and with all nations."

That gigantic system of fleets and armies, the creation of which was due to Lincoln, was closing tight around the dying Confederacy. Five weeks after the inauguration Lee surrendered, and the war was virtually at an end. What was to come after was inevitably the overshadowing topic of the hour. Many anecdotes represent Lincoln, in these last few days of his life, as possessed by a high though melancholy mood of extreme mercy. Therefore, much has been inferred from the following words, in his last public address, made on the night of the 11th of April: "In the present situation, as the phrase goes, it may be my duty to make some new announcement to the people of the South. I am considering and shall not fail to act when action shall be proper."

What was to be done for the South, what treatment should be accorded the Southern leaders, engrossed the President and his Cabinet at the meeting on the 14th of April, which was destined to be their last. Secretary Welles has preserved the spirit of the meeting in a striking anecdote. Lincoln said that no one need expect he would "take any part in hanging or killing those men, even the worst of them. Frighten them out of the country, open the gates, let down the bars, scare them off;" said he, throwing up his hands as if scaring sheep. "Enough lives have been sacrificed; we must extinguish our resentments if we expect harmony and union."

While Lincoln was thus arming himself with a valiant mercy, a band of conspirators at an obscure boardinghouse in Washington were planning his assassination. Their leader was John Wilkes Booth, an actor, brother of the much abler Edwin Booth. There seems little doubt that he was insane. Around him gathered a small group of visionary extremists in whom much brooding upon Southern wrongs had produced an unbalanced condition. Only a morbid interest can attach today to the strange cunning with which Booth laid his plans, thinking of himself all the while as a reincarnation of the Roman Brutus.

On the night of the 14th of April, the President attended a performance of "Our American Cousin". While the play was in progress, Booth stole into the President's box, came close behind him, and shot him through the head. Lincoln never spoke again and, shortly after seven next morning, ceased breathing.

At the same time, a futile attempt was made upon the life of Seward. Booth temporarily escaped. Later he was overtaken and shot. His accomplices were hanged.

The passage of sixty years has proved fully necessary to the placing of Lincoln in historic perspective. No President, in his own time, with the possible exception of Washington, was so bitterly hated and so fiercely reviled. On the other hand, none has been the object of such intemperate hero-worship. However, the greatest of the land were, in the main, quick to see him in perspective and to recognize his historic significance. It is recorded of Davis that in after days he paid a beautiful tribute to Lincoln and said, "Next to the destruction of the Confederacy, the death of Abraham Lincoln was the darkest day the South has known."

BIBLIOGRAPHICAL NOTE

There are two general histories, of conspicuous ability, that deal with this period:

J. F. Rhodes, "History of the United States from the Compromise of 1850", 7 vols. (1893-1906), and J. B. McMaster, "History of the People of the United States", 7 vols. (1883-1912). McMaster has the more "modern" point of view and is excellent but dry, without any sense of narrative. Rhodes has a somewhat older point of view. For example, he makes only a casual reference, in a quotation, to the munitions problem of 1861, though analyzing with great force and candor such constitutional issues as the arrests under the suspension of the writ of habeas corpus. The other strong points in his work are its sense of narrative, its freedom from hero-worship, its independence of conventional views of Northern leaders. As to the South, it suffers from a certain Narrowness of vision due to the comparative scantiness of the material used. The same may be said of McMaster.

For Lincoln, there is no adequate brief biography. Perhaps the best is the most recent, "Abraham Lincoln", by Lord Charnwood ("Makers of the Nineteenth Century", 1917). It has a kind of cool detachment that hardly any biographer had shown previously, and yet this coolness is joined with extreme admiration. Short biographies worth considering are John T. Morse, Jr., Abraham Lincoln ("American Statesmen" Series, 2 vols., 1893), and Ida M. Tarbell, "Life of Abraham Lincoln", 2 vols. (1900). The official biography is in ten volumes, "Abraham Lincoln, a History", by his secretaries, John G. Nicolay and John Hay (1890). It is a priceless document and as such is little likely to be forgotten. But its events are so numerous that they swamp the figure of Lincoln and yet are not numerous enough to constitute a definitive history of the times. It is wholly eulogistic. The same authors edited "The Writings of Abraham Lincoln" (Biographical Edition, 2 vols., 1894), which has since been expanded (1905) and now fills twelve volumes. It is the definitive presentation of Lincoln's mind. A book much sought after by his enemies is William Henry Herndon and Jesse William Weik, "The History and Personal Recollections of Abraham Lincoln", 8 vols. (1889; unexpurgated edition). It contains about all we know of his early life and paints a picture of sordid ugliness. Its reliability has been disputed. No study of Lincoln is complete unless one has marched through the "Diary" of Gideon Welles, Secretary of the Navy, 3 vols. (1911), which is our most important document showing Lincoln in his Cabinet. Important sidelights on his character and development are shown in Ward Hill Lamon, "Recollections of Lincoln" (1911); David Homer Bates, "Lincoln in the Telegraph Office" (1907); and Frederick Trevor Hill, "Lincoln as a Lawyer" (1906). A bibliography of Lincoln is in the twelfth volume of the latest edition of the "Writings".

The lesser statesmen of the time, both Northern and Southern, still, as a rule, await proper treatment by detached biographers. Two Northerners have had such treatment, in Allen Johnson's "Stephen A. Douglas" (1908), and Frederic Bancroft's "Life of William H. Seward", 2 vols. (1900). Good, but without the requisite detachment, is Moorfield Storey's "Charles Sumner", ("American Statesmen Series", 1900). With similar excellences but with the same defect, though still the best in its field, is Albert Bushnell Hart's "Salmon P. Chase" ("American Statesmen Series", 1899). Among the Southern statesmen involved in the events of this volume, only the President of the Confederacy has received adequate reconsideration in recent years, in William E. Dodd's "Jefferson Davis" (1907). The latest life of "Robert Toombs", by Ulrich B. Phillips (1914), is not definitive, but the best extant. The great need for adequate lives of Stephens and Yancey is not at all met by the obsolete works—R. M. Johnston and W. M. Browne, "Life of Alexander H. Stephens" (1878), and J. W. Du Bose, "The Life and Times of William Lowndes Yancey" (1892). There is a brief biography of Stephens by Louis Pendleton, in the "American Crisis Biographies". Most of the remaining biographies of the period, whether Northern or Southern, are either too superficial or too partisan to be recommended for general use. Almost alone in their way are the delightful "Confederate Portraits", by Gamaliel Bradford (1914), and the same author's "Union Portraits "(1916).

Upon conditions in the North during the war there is a vast amount of material; but little is accessible to the general reader. A book of great value is Emerson Fite's Social and Industrial Conditions in the North during the Civil War (1910). Out of unnumbered books of reminiscence, one stands forth for the sincerity of its disinterested, if sharp, observation—W. H. Russell's "My Diary North and South" (1868). Two newspapers are invaluable: The "New York Tribune" for a version of events as seen by the war party, "The New York Herald "for the opposite point of view; the Chicago papers are also important, chiefly the "Times" and "Tribune"; the "Republican "of Springfield, Mass., had begun its distinguished career, while the "Journal" and "Advertiser" of Boston revealed Eastern New England. For the Southern point of view, no papers are more important than the Richmond "Examiner", the Charleston "Mercury", and the New Orleans "Picayune". Financial and economic problems are well summed up in D. R. Dewey's "Financial History of the United States" (3d edition, 1907), and in E. P. Oberholzer's "Jay Cooks", 2 vols. (1907). Foreign affairs are summarized adequately in C. F. Adams's "Charles Francis Adams" ("American Statesmen Series", 1900), John Bigelow's "France and the Confederate Navy" (1888), A. P. Martin's "Maximilian in Mexico" (1914), and John Bassett Moore's "Digest of International Law", 8 vols. (1906).

The documents of the period ranging from newspapers to presidential messages are not likely to be considered by the general reader, but if given a fair chance will prove fascinating. Besides the biographical edition of Lincoln's Writings, should be named, first of all, "The Congressional Globe" for debates in Congress; the "Statutes at Large"; the "Executive Documents", published by the Government and containing a great number of reports; and the enormous collection issued by the War Department under the title "Official Records of the Union and Confederate Armies", 128 vols. (1880-1901), especially the groups of volumes known as second and third series.

www.ingramcontent.com/pod-product-compliance
Lightning Source LLC
Chambersburg PA
CBHW051806040426
42446CB00007B/536